THE GATES OF HELL

*

A vivid book on the most dangerous and uncomfortable convoy route in the last war—the trip to Murmansk. Ewart Brookes gives a remarkable account of what the escort ships and their charges had to endure. At the heart of this stirring book is the author's indictment that lives were needlessly endangered by the orders of men thousands of miles away from the scene of the action.

Also in Arrow Books by Ewart Brookes

Destroyer
Proud Waters

Ewart Brookes

The Gates of Hell

ARROW BOOKS

ARROW BOOKS LTD
3 Fitzroy Square, London W1

AN IMPRINT OF THE HUTCHINSON GROUP

London Melbourne Sydney Auckland
Wellington Johannesburg Cape Town
and agencies throughout the world

First published by
Jarrolds Publishers (London) Ltd 1960
Arrow edition 1962
This new edition 1973

This book is published at a net price and supplied subject to the Publishers Association Standard Condition of Sale registered under the Restrictive Trade Practices Act 1956

Made and printed in Great Britain
by The Anchor Press Ltd,
Tiptree, Essex

ISBN 0 09 906950 4

ACKNOWLEDGEMENTS

My thanks are due to many people for their assistance and guidance in producing this narrative: to The Lords Commissioners of the Admiralty; Mr. M. Ellis of the Department of the Chief of Naval Information for his 'pilotage' through various departments; Rear Admiral R. St. V. Sherbrooke, VC, CB, DSO (and Mrs. Sherbrooke); Captain Jack Broome, DSC; Godfrey Winn for permitting me to use extracts from his *PQ 17* and Dudley Pope for extracts from *73 North*.

I owe my thanks to my friend and colleague Bernard Hall for anecdotes of his trips in H.M.S. *Scylla*.

Also to Admiral of the Fleet Lord Fraser, GCB, KBE, for the foreword.

I also owe thanks to two other esteemed gentlemen. To my friend 'Bill' Crumley, late Naval Correspondent, *Daily Express*, for considerable material he had collected over the years on the German aspects of the war and to Admiral Robert L. Burnett, GCB, KCB, DSO, who was patiently answering questions by post. We were to have met on one of his visits to London.

We never did. Both he and Crumley passed over the river into the shade of the trees while the book was in preparation.

E.B.

London

MAP

On page 192 is a map showing the course of convoys PQ17 and JW51B

ILLUSTRATIONS

Between pages 96 and 97

FOREWORD

FROM

Admiral of the Fleet Lord Fraser
of North Cape, GCB, KBE

My Dear Brookes,

It was indeed kind of you to send me a copy of your book and I do congratulate you, not only on bringing forward the story of the Arctic convoys, but on the vivid writing.

You have done full justice to all who served in those waters.

I know from reading it that you will have great success with your book. My best wishes to you.

I know so well all those you mention including Broome, Sherbrooke and Burnett (unfortunately now departed from us).

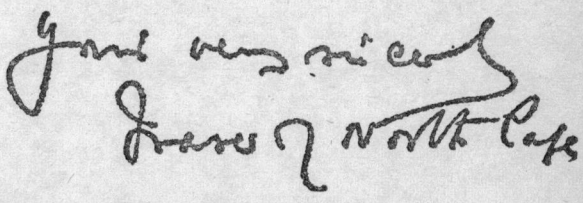

Yours very sincerely
Fraser of North Cape

AUTHOR'S NOTE

I MAKE no apology for the tinge of indignation which intrudes into this foreword.

A little while ago I was talking to some youngsters. Most of them were in their middle 'teens, laying assault to the General Certificate of Education—in a word, they were lively intelligent youngsters. Out of the blue—literally because we were lying on our backs in the sun watching planes threading the sky—I asked them if they knew anything about PQ17 or JW51B or Kola.

Now, I asked because almost without exception they had been arguing long and informatively about the various marks of Spitfire, Hurricane, Beaufort, Mosquito, JU88, Mustang and other lethal planes right up to the latest faster-than-sound jobs. Of bombers, raids, air fights and air aces they were almost word perfect. But Arctic convoys? They had only a very superficial knowledge of convoys at all, but had never heard of those which sailed to Russia during the last war.

Later, in a thoughtful mood, I posed the question to some older people, some of whom had served in the war. One of them hazarded a guess that PQ17 and JW51B were part of the formula for the latest antibiotic, an improved form of penicillin; another suggested that they might be a code for atomic missiles.

Perhaps they are not to blame. At the time it was all happening the Free World was subjected to a rightly imposed censorship. There were of course occasional guarded references in the newspapers to Arctic convoys, but so scant that they were insufficient to make any impact on the public mind, and the Royal Navy did not feel quite the same about uniformed Press Relations and Public Relations officers as did the other Services. While men ranking up to wing-commander rightly proclaimed the exploits of the RAF, and Army personnel, up to the rank of full colonel, publicized the work of the soldiers, I think I am correct in saying that only a small handful of lieutenant-commanders were appointed as naval PROs—and they were certainly not overworked.

So, virtually unsung, thousands of men in hundreds of ships laboured across the roof of the world under conditions which defy adequate description. For four years they ferried almost every kind of war material to an ally who treated their efforts with scorn, and who—like Oliver Twist—demanded more but was not prepared to furnish more than minute and reluctant co-operation.

During those long and gruelling four years the Germans held all the advantages. In winter-time our men suffered cold and weariness in the unending nights, suffered it beyond endurance and yet went on enduring. In the long summer nights, when there was no brief respite of darkness to bring relief, the convoys were hammered by U-boats and aircraft for days on end. Losses in merchant ships were dreadfully heavy, and Royal Navy escorts, too, had their gaps, saddening gaps, at a time when every ship was worth treble its weight in gold.

Ironically, the Germans' failure entirely to stop the convoys led ultimately to Hitler having one of his celebrated brainstorms; and the German pocket-battleships and heavy cruisers (which had been a constant threat throughout) were relegated to the status of floating barracks, or were decommissioned. To tell the complete story of the Arctic convoys would require several volumes. Each convoy in itself was an epic in the truest sense of the word, an epic both glorious and tragic. Within self-imposed limits I have tried in the following pages to paint a picture on a wide canvas. I have limned in the first tentative sailings across the roof of the world, and then the later sailings when the convoys had, quite literally, to be fought through fire and blood—to the end when they sailed almost arrogantly, dragging their coattails across the noses of the Germans.

Throughout this narrative it becomes apparent that the long-distance planners, seated around broad tables a couple of thousand miles away, obviously thought they knew better than the man on the spot. . . . And the men in the ships suffered because of this assumption; because of it they had to die, some of them unnecessarily. They had been given orders, and they obeyed.

One

AS THE grey-pink flush of the false dawn faded from the sky over eastern Poland on the morning of 22 June 1941, Russian soldiers in their rough block-houses heard the concerted roar of engines burst into life in front of them.

The attack had begun. Germany was making war against Russia. The paper-thin German-Soviet Pact of 1939, conceived in sardonic cynicism, signed in irony, had served its purpose! With rage concealed behind the mask of a smile, Hitler had accepted Russia's rape of fallen Poland and had allowed Stalin's troops to occupy parts of eastern Poland—but only until such time as once more his patience was exhausted and he could 'rectify the position'. In the meantime the lightning campaign of twenty days which had wiped out Poland, seen the overrunning of Norway, the occupation of Holland and Denmark and the crashing defeat of the Anglo-French armies had fully occupied Hitler's mind.

By the summer of 1940 he was in possession of all Europe—or all of it that mattered—with the exception of Italy and Spain. In December (Boxing Day to be precise) Hitler announced to his staff that the German armed forces must be prepared, even before the end of the war against England, to overthrow Russia in a rapid campaign. The operation was to be planned under the title Operation Barbarossa forthwith.

Stalin had caused Hitler some uneasiness in July 1940, as indeed Hitler in his turn had given Stalin food for deep thought. The increasing German influence in the Balkans provoked Stalin into moving into the Baltic states of Latvia, Lithuania and Estonia. Hitler became thoughtfully conscious of the unpleasant proximity of Russian troops to the homeland. He knew, too, of the Russian capacity for selling space to gain time, but was reluctant to force the issue immediately, as he would be then engaged on two fronts—an eastern and a western—at the same time. It is true that his western front was then no more than a holding front, but it nevertheless had to be held.

The stupid British, led by that 'drunkard Churchill', had flatly, even arrogantly, refused to consider a bartered peace whereby England and her possessions would be left inviolate in return for a free hand against Russia. All through the hot summer of that year 1940 and into the autumn, while his all-powerful air force hammered at Britain, Hitler still clung to the hope that—rather than face a protracted war—this country would seek an honourable peace. By the time he realized that he had misjudged the temper of the British, the winter was too close to do more than think of eliminating Russia. So at a conference which spread over Christmas 1940, Hitler committed his staff to planning war against Russia.

By the beginning of June 1941 the vast German army, its triumphs resting new on its brow, was ready. It was to be no long-drawn-out campaign. Six weeks, Hitler estimated, would see the affair all over, apart from trimming up the untidy ends, so there were no preparations for winter warfare. German tanks and Stuka dive-bombers would repeat on a larger canvas the picture of flame and destruction which they had painted across Poland and France.

On the morning of 22 June 1941 the German army and air force rolled into action. At the outset it looked as if the pattern was to be repeated. The Russian armies reeled back, and the wide advances made by the invaders seemed to make the estimate of six weeks unnecessarily cautious.

From the White Sea to the Crimea the Russians pulled back, leaving only a completely scorched earth for the advancing German armies. The stupendous sacrifices by the Russian armies slowed down the enemy, until, halted on the threshold of the vast production areas in Russia, the Germans reluctantly had to accept the unpalatable fact that they were committed to a campaign extending at least into one winter. Russian production of war material was not equal, at that stage, to meet the demands of its armies and so it appealed for outside help.

That other vast workshop of production, America, was rapidly gearing itself for war on a scale never even dreamed of two or three years previously. Not only was it producing in an ever-growing stream for its own forces, now at grips with the Japanese, but it was providing in a large measure for the British. Astutely, Churchill and Roosevelt recognized that the more help they could afford to send to Russia the greater would be the chance of ultimate defeat of the enemy in the West and in the Near East. To promise help, and to get the material to Russia, were two different kettles of fish.

One way would be the long haul around the Cape, up to the Persian Gulf and by the single tenuous line from Teheran. A slender link indeed. The alternative was by ship across the roof of the world.

Study a large-scale map of the Barents Sea or, better still, an even larger map which includes those vast areas of water which extend from Greenland, Iceland, south of Spitzbergen, Bear Island, Franz Josef Land, that long curved finger of an island, Novaya Zemlya, which points north, splitting the Barents Sea from the Kara Sea. Millions of square miles of water in which to sail convoys, room in which to manœuvre a fleet of ships. In peace-time ships sailed from Archangel, Murmansk and Kola, hugged the coast until they rounded North Cape and began threading the fiords of Norway.

Trawlers of the great maritime nations braved the waters around Bear Island and Iceland in search of better quality fish; an occasional supply-ship in summer thrust northwards to Spitzbergen. . . . In winter-time the ice creeps down until it almost touches Bear Island; in summer it retreats until a passage north of that bleak little dot is possible, even as far northwards as that ironically named black sentinel, Hope Island, south of Spitzbergen. The tactical problem facing those who would have to organize convoys along that route was basically the same as that which faced every other convoy sailing in war-time. Re-route, wriggle and twist it as one might, ultimately it would have to pass a focal-point where an enemy would be waiting for it.

In this instance it was the comparatively narrow gap between Bear Island and North Cape, the tip of Norway. After the fall of Norway the Germans lost no time in creating a 'fleet in being' near North Cape, but that time it was not for the purpose of attacking convoys—such a thing was undreamed of then. The Germans merely visualized the advantages of having pocket-battleships and heavy cruisers so much nearer a point from which they could break out into the North Atlantic without the greater risk of being detected by our patrols.

The six weeks or so in which Hitler estimated that he would overrun Russia had elapsed, and it became obvious that he was committed to at least one winter of gruelling winter warfare. Churchill and Roosevelt had promised all-out aid. Now came the task of implementing that promise. The world wondered how it could be done, even wondered if it could be done. Speaking to the House of Commons early in September, Mr. Churchill said:

'From the moment, now eighty days ago, when Russia was attacked, we have cast about for every means of giving the most speedy and effective help to our new allies.

'The need is urgent and the scale heavy. . . . The study of the whole procedure has been ceaselessly proceeding here and in the United States, and we are awaiting the arrival of the American Mission under Mr. [Averell] Harriman.' Then came the name of the man who was to lead the British mission to Moscow, to discuss the ways and means and quantities of material. 'Lord Beaverbrook has already visited the United States and has been in the closest conference with the President, his advisers and officers.'

Sitting in the Distinguished Visitors' Gallery in the House

of Commons the Russian Ambassador to Great Britain, Mr. Maisky, sat back and smiled. Here was one man, the ambassador must have thought, who will do something more than talk, here is one man who will again cut through protocol, ruthlessly wipe away objections and eliminate red tape and will get things done as he had when Great Britain, down to its last few planes in the summer of 1940, found itself spurred, cajoled and bullied into producing more when pundits said more could not be produced. . . .

Mr. Churchill went on to give this sombre warning: 'We must be prepared for heavy sacrifices in the munitions field to meet the needs of Russia. Everything we give to Russia will be subtracted from what we are making ourselves or, in part at least, from what would have been sent us by the United States.' The road indeed was to be hard. We were striving to meet the ever-increasing demands of our own forces—tanks, vehicles, munitions, ships and every conceivable form of war-supplies—and we were about to pledge all-out help to Russia from that supply!

Within a week the constitution of the joint American-British Mission was made known. Lord Beaverbrook, Minister of Supply, headed the British contingent. With him was to go Captain H. H. Balfour, Parliamentary Under-Secretary for Air, Major-General Sir Hastings Ismay, senior staff officer of the Ministry of Defence, Major-General G. N. Macready, Assistant Chief of the Imperial General Staff. Already in Moscow were Lieutenant-General F. N. Mason-Macfarlane, Rear-Admiral G. J. A. Miles and Air Vice-Marshal A. C. Collier. On the American side were Lease-lend 'expediter' Harriman, Major-General James

Burns, Major-General George H. Brett, Mr. William L. Batt and Admiral W. H. Standley.

On the eve of his departure, early in September 1941, Lord Beaverbrook left the following message for the factory workers who were already going flat out in ever-increasing production:

'I am on my way, taking with me to Moscow your pledge and promise to the soldiers and workers of Russia. I leave you—each one of you—responsible for production results during my absence, and I rely on you to see that the promise I make on your behalf will be fulfilled. . . .

'Let me tell the Russians that in the last days of September you devoted yourselves to their needs—that you built more tanks than ever before in the history of our country.'

And a few nights later the cruiser *London*, carrying the joint Mission, turned her lean grey bows northwards and plunged into a head sea, sailing across the roof of the world on a track which later was to be the heartbreak course for convoy after convoy. No time was wasted. The Russians stated their needs, the Mission outlined in detail what they could supply, and almost before the ink was dry the first convoy was already on its way with planes. Lord Beaverbrook returned, a promise made. Ships then still in American ports were being loaded at top speed, ships still at sea were being earmarked for convoys to Russia. And in that bleak, wind-swept bastion Scapa Flow the C-in-C Home Fleet, Admiral Sir John Tovey, began to take stock.

To implement Beaverbrook's promise, to push through—to fight through, if necessary—the convoys which would have to sail was going to impose on the C-in-C's thinly stretched resources a strain which in the twinkling of an eye could bring it to breaking-point. His precious escort ships, the destroyers, the corvettes, fleet minesweepers (used for anything but minesweeping) and armed asdic trawlers were already heavily committed to sparsely guarded Atlantic convoys. His heavier ships, 6-inch and 8-inch cruisers, had to be ever ready to race forth in search of a German raider.

The load was going to increase—nobody visualized then to what extent. But a promise had been made, and so far as human endeavour could achieve in naval ships it would be carried out. Orders would be brusque, dogmatic. 'Escorts will rendezvous with convoy. . . .' Many men would die, many ships would be sunk, without questioning why. The first two or three convoys sailed, headed north from Loch Ewe to Iceland, north again towards Bear Island then eastwards for the Russian ports. And they arrived safely. No patrolling U-boat had detected them; no wide-flying aircraft spotted them to flash back their course and speed. But nobody, least of all the men on the escort ships, believed for one moment that this sort of thing would last.

And it didn't.

Two

THAT the Germans would sooner or later commit surface craft to an attack on a convoy was generally accepted. The stage was admirably prepared for such an excursion. It was also shrewdly deducted that if and when such an attack came it would be on, or east of, a line drawn from Bear Island and North Cape—and the White Sea. West of that the Germans would be heading into waters where the chances of their taking a mauling were appreciably increased.

The first surface attack, in fact, came against PQ6, a convoy of seven ships which sailed from Iceland on 8 December 1941. It was bound for Kola Inlet. The ocean escort handed over the intact convoy to a local escort of British fleet minesweepers which jealously shepherded seven ships for the last few miles of their voyage. Suddenly two of the sweepers, *Speedy* and *Hazard*, saw the flashes of gun-fire in the gloom north of them. *Speedy* was almost immediately hit—her mast was shot away and both her 4-inch guns were hit.

The two sweepers were completely outgunned. The German destroyers which were shooting at them mounted 5.1-inch guns, and were nearly twice as fast. The damaged *Speedy* and the *Hazard* turned away to the south, making smoke to cover the convoy, while the remainder of the escort, all the escorting fleet sweepers, hastened to insert themselves between the raiding German destroyers and the convoy. The Germans, possibly suspecting a trap, turned away from the small force of escorting ships. Had they continued their thrust they could have destroyed, first, all the escort by sheer weight of armament, then closed in on the convoy and could have sunk many of the ships in it. Instead, they turned away into the shrouding gloom.

That lack of final thrust became a characteristic of most of the German surface-craft raids on subsequent convoys. There were to be many occasions when resolution and dash would have presented to the Germans an opportunity for soul-shaking disaster to escort and convoy. Even U-boats and aircraft seemed content to lie in wait off Kola until a convoy was on the point of dispersing before staging an attack. At least, this was so in the earlier winter days of the first convoys. Somebody in authority later assured the Prime Minister that were the situation reversed and the Royal Navy was attacking the convoys, then not one of them would have got through.

The Germans, of course, were not yet fully alive to the amount of traffic which was steaming across the roof of the world in hours of almost continuous darkness. They had submarines patrolling west of Bear Island, off Iceland and other parts of the frozen north; but their preoccupation was to detect any aggressive movement by the Home Fleet in the direction of a strike against their bases in north Norway.

Undoubtedly their Intelligence had reported the movements of convoys, and shrewdly estimated their destination—but the extent of the traffic and the frequency of the convoys were yet to become so apparent to them that it was obvious that supplying Russia was becoming a major and sustained operation. So the earlier convoys got through without any serious punishment. Even so, they were given an escort which would make any Senior Officer escort on a Western Ocean convoy, or one to Freetown, green with envy. Convoys were sailing those routes with one or two destroyers, four corvettes and a trawler.

One instance will serve to illustrate the tragic paucity of escort ships. A convoy sailed for West Africa, down through U-boat alley, with an escort of four little corvettes—a mass of shipping five or six miles across the front and three or four miles deep! With one corvette to each side U-boats could, and did, attack with impunity. It was asking the impossible to expect the corvettes to guard all points. In the convoy in question a seven-days' fight raged around it and thirteen ships were lost, half the convoy, and not one U-boat was sunk.

The convoys to Russia were, by such standards, heavily escorted. It was recognized, of course, that providing Russia with an increasing quantity of supplies was a major priority, ranking with the task of preventing Germany and Japan joining somewhere in the East, and to check Japan's headlong dash for India and Australia and ultimately New Zealand. But human endeavour was not enough: ships were in short supply and were getting scarcer, the U-boats were sinking faster than our all-out shipyards could build. It took a year to build a ship and about five minutes to blow her into oblivion. And the same applied to escort ships, corvettes, frigates and destroyers.

One sometimes wonders whether the strident, pink politicians who were about that time hysterically screaming 'What about a Second Front to help Russia?' had any conception of the immensity of the problem, or of the task being undertaken by the merchant ships and their escorts through the frozen north. I doubt it. It was a pity that a few of them were not invited to sail in one such convoy and so experience at first hand what it was like. Probably such a gesture would have failed anyway: the only political observers I ever saw on board warships were far more preoccupied with the duty-free cigarettes and the cheapness of the pink gins than in naval operations in comparatively safe waters.

With the hours of darkness increasing in our favour we started to enlarge the weight of the convoys. PQ7 sailed in two parts on 31 December 1941 and 8 January 1942. The first part comprised two ships (tankers), capable of a respectable turn of speed, with additional cargo lashed on deck, and the second part was made up of nine ships. The two tankers arrived without being spotted; but the second part, when practically home, lost one ship and had another damaged by a mine off Kola Inlet, which, however, managed to get in.

Those German minefields were a sore point with the PQ and QP convoys and escorts. We were having a grim battle with German mine-laying around our own ports. Contact, magnetic and acoustic mines were closing ports and estuaries and giving us a major problem. Our minesweeping forces were being stretched to their limits owing to the immensity of the task and the shortage of ships.

To deal with the minefields off Kola and the other ports we sent precious minesweepers to the Russians, together with experts who were to show them how to cope with the successive types being constantly introduced by the Germans. After accepting the ships, the Russians showed a marked inclination to ignore such tasks as minesweeping, and more than one ship, having battled through vile weather, and successfully fought off dive-bombers and torpedo-bombers and avoided U-boats, fell victims to mines when almost at the end of the run. Eventually, thoroughly exasperated at this quite incomprehensible Russian attitude, we sent a couple of flotillas of minesweepers to deal with the problem our way, and the Russians treated the crews of them with marked hostility. But the mines were swept.

Escorting the second part of PQ7 was the destroyer *Matabele*, one of the large 'Tribals' which wrote history from the Arctic to the Pacific before they nearly all disappeared.

And *Matabele* was sunk on 17 January east of Bear Island. A rescue ship raced towards her and reached her in a few minutes. There were men in the water, their heads held above it by their lifebelts, men who stared back at their rescuers, with unblinking, unseeing eyes, men who bobbed about in the waves, in groups, as if they were taking part in some grotesque square dance. . . . But all of them were dead. Frozen in little more time than it takes to boil an egg. Two *Matabele* men alone survived.

The next convoys were larger. PQ9 formed up at Iceland, ten ships strong, and PQ11 was built at Loch Ewe with thirteen ships. They both sailed on 1 February, but because of their relative starting-points would be five days or so apart. They both crept north and east, and eventually eastward in weather that defies adequate description. They were lashed by gales, and the spray and snow, freezing into solid masses as it fell, turned the ships into fantastic icing-sugared shapes which bore no resemblance to ships, and on them men lived—or barely existed. And the convoys were not discovered. This, however, was hardly surprising, for visibility from the conning tower of a U-boat in that weather was zero minus. In any event, as Admiral Tovey acidly commented, the U-boats merely had to wait in the White Sea, lie off Kola Inlet and savage the convoys as they arrived.

This, too, was a sore point. Admiral Tovey felt that as we had undertaken the immense task of getting the convoys through, the Russians might at least take some steps to make those close waters untenable to German submarines. They had destroyers available, and in fact the minesweepers we had given them were equipped with asdic and depth-charges and had the speed and punch to attack a submarine. He also felt that at the end of the voyage the Russians should provide some sort of fighter cover for the convoys.

So strongly did he feel about this that he sent Admiral H. M. Burrough in the cruiser *Nigeria* to Kola Inlet to press the need, and to cover the convoys between Bear Island and

Kola. Admiral Burrough was probably one of the first to meet that conclusive and endlessly repeated word: *Niet!*

From the pattern which had begun to formulate, it seemed obvious that any attack on a convoy by heavy surface units would come from Bear Island eastward.

Three

THE virtual starting- and finishing-points of the convoys, Iceland, were known to the Germans. Submarines could shadow and harry a convoy from Iceland to Kola Inlet. Another threat began to build itself up: it was known that the Germans had withdrawn bomber forces from the Russian front to build up a striking-force in north Norway, and they were also adding torpedo-bombers to it. They, too, could attack when the convoy was abeam of Bear Island and eastward of it.

The growing threat of an attack by heavy surface ships was an additional burden, but Admiral Tovey felt that they would not be committed to an action when the convoy was still sailing northwards from Iceland, in an arena where they might be tackled by our heavy covering force. Subsequent events showed that he was not far off the mark. The long hours of darkness were still on our side. The convoys could sail with only three or four hours of daylight each day, added to which gales and snowstorms followed each other with increasing frequency and severity.

So on 1 February two convoys sailed hard on each other's heels. PQ9 and PQ10 sailed from Iceland—a convoy of ten ships in two parts—and PQ11 from Loch Ewe started out on the same day, thirteen ships strong. By 9 February, what with escorts, covering forces and the three convoys, the waters between Iceland and the Barents Sea were quite heavily populated with ships slamming into an almost endless succession of 'concealing' gales. They got through without being located and, apart from damage by the weather, there were no casualties.

Nobody but the wildest optimists visualized this unscathed sailing of convoys going on endlessly. Sooner or later there would be a concerted attack on a convoy by submarines, aircraft and—it was more than a possibility—pocket-battleships and heavy cruisers. And it nearly came to pass.

PQ12, a convoy of sixteen ships, sailed from Iceland on 1 March; and a return convoy of ships in ballast (some of them being ships from PQ convoys 7, 8, 9, 10 and 11) started on its homeward journey. That was convoy QP8. Five days later the submarine *Seawolf*, pitching and plunging on her lonely and dangerous patrol off Norway, reported that enemy surface craft had sailed from Trondhjem. *Tirpitz* was out! She had sailed, under Admiral Ciliax, with three destroyers on the afternoon of the 5th, to be spotted next morning by *Seawolf*.

At the same time a German plane reported PQ12 and proceeded to shadow it, well out of gun-range. Then fate played one of its unpredictable tricks. Snow and fog shut down over the convoy so that it was almost impossible to see the ship ahead, and the frustrated plane was completely blinded. Instead of being able to home *Tirpitz* and her destroyers on to the convoy, it could not even report whether the convoy was maintaining the same course and speed. So *Tirpitz* had to begin a search.

In the meantime battleships *King George V*, *Duke of York*, *Renown*, the aircraft-carrier *Victorious*, the cruiser *Berwick* and twelve destroyers had sailed from Scapa to make a wide sweep south of the convoy routes. Visibility was still atrocious, but the stage was set for a destructive and conclusive battle. *Tirpitz*, groping northwards for the convoy, and the heavy British ships searching for her were at one time actually within a little more than one hour's steaming time from each other.

King George V and her consorts knew the route and approximate position of the convoy, and maintained their sweep to keep south of it to intercept *Tirpitz*. The German ship, guessing at the convoy's whereabouts, steamed north and actually passed between the two convoys and probed farther north. She sailed a few miles astern of the convoy PQ12 and ahead of QP8, and eventually turned and sailed south. So *Tirpitz* twice cut the convoy route without locating either. It is a purely academic question as to what would have happened had (1) PQ12 been a knot or two slower, or (2) QP8 been a knot or two faster. *Tirpitz* would have found them, would undoubtedly have done a tremendous amount of damage to one or both before *King George V* and avenging forces would have caught up with her, as they would undoubtedly have done.

Tirpitz, still working on the assumption that she had cut the convoy route before PQ12 had arrived, detached her destroyers on the morning of the 7th and sent them on a fast sweep to the north to search for it while she turned and steamed north of *King George V* and the others, but parallel to their course. *Tirpitz* was nearer jeopardy for those couple of hours than she ever could have dreamed possible.

The British heavy force assumed *Tirpitz* was still south of them, and on that assumption rightly steamed to protect the convoy routes. Actually she was alone and north of them—an hour's steaming time away. Her searching destroyers caught up with a Russian straggler from PQ12 and summarily sank it, but not before it got off a garbled signal which did not give a clear position. It was impossible to tell whether the victim was east or west of PQ12, or for that matter north or south. Finally the destroyers rejoined *Tirpitz* and the force turned south with its one solitary scalp dangling from its belt instead of leaving behind a badly mauled convoy.

One of the few clear breaks in the weather came and *Victorious* flew off some torpedo-carrying Albacores. Almost at the end of their sweep they discovered *Tirpitz* racing homewards and attacked, but missed her. Again the dice fell right for *Tirpitz*. Had one of the torpedoes got home and slowed her down, she would have still been within reach of *King George V* and her consorts. . . . And the primary causes for all this naval activity—PQ12 and QP8—arrived at their destinations safely.

But by now it was obvious that an integral part of any PQ and QP convoy-planning would involve the disposal of sufficient heavy surface craft to meet an ever-present threat of an attack by German battleships and cruisers on the destroyers. This was indeed a heavy task when the calls upon the Royal Navy for ships of every description was stretching its resources to the utmost. Furthermore, the merchant ships in the convoys, and the precious cargoes they carried, were being sacrificed by the United States and ourselves when every ship and every ounce of cargo they carried were vital to our own desperate needs. Nevertheless, planning went on for more and larger convoys which by now would have to sail in periods when the hours of daylight would be lengthening.

PQ13 sailed from Reykjavik on 21 March. There were nineteen ships in this convoy, and at the same time QP9 which was despatched from Murmansk for the homeward run was also nineteen ships strong. The reason for sailing the homeward and outward convoys on or about the same dates was simple. They would cross one another in the vicinity of Bear Island where the cruiser covering force and, if necessary—if the threat became alive enough—a heavy force could be sailed to guard the route and so cover both convoys in the most dangerous area. The Germans by now had assembled their U-boats and aircraft for stronger attacks. QP9 suffered a few desultory attacks by U-boats and planes, but the close escorts and the merchant-ships' gunners dealt adequately with them. It could be assumed that the Germans were attacking the empty returning ships more by way of target practice than anything else. They were to concentrate with deadly intent on the loaded ships with their deck cargoes of crated bombers, tanks and trucks, and vital stores in their holds.

Indeed, QP9's escort showed a dividend. The fleet minesweeper *Sharpshooter* detected, attacked and sank U-655 as the submarine was rather arrogantly closing in to the convoy with the intention of fanning it with torpedoes. But PQ13 ran into real trouble. On the morning of the 24th a gale started which built itself up to frightening proportions. It blew for three days and nights, the wind never dropping below a strident shriek. Ships laboured up creaming mountainous seas, slipping down the other side only to start the process over and over again. To add to the trouble, most of the ships, with bulky cargoes lashed on their decks, steered badly. Vicious, blinding snow-squalls added to the terror, and ship after ship carried the signal 'Not under control'. Collisions were averted by a matter of feet, as masters strove to turn their ships to an easier course.

And on the fourth day, when the wind abated to a threatening growl, not one ship remained in sight of another —they were scattered over hundreds of miles of grey, foam-flecked sea—and the cruiser *Trinidad* and her accompanying destroyers found themselves screening a convoy which did not exist. So for the escorts, fleet sweepers, destroyers, corvettes and asdic trawlers began a heartbreaking task—that of rounding up a scattered convoy of nineteen ships without one single craft being in sight. This task had to be done when the crews of the escorts, wearied beyond description, just wanted to close their eyes, if only for a brief spell, and sleep.

On the 28th, German aircraft patrolling wide found for themselves a feast to gladden their hearts. Labouring over the uneasy seas, and with no escorts in sight, were scattered merchant ships—fat, heavily laden merchant ships, scattered like frightened sheep. And not a pugnacious fire-spitting escort in sight! They joyfully called up their friends and buckled down to their task. They sank two before merciful snow-squalls and driving rain robbed them of visibility. Three German destroyers which had sailed on the tail-end of the gale on the afternoon of the 28th forayed north and picked up a Panamanian straggler. Before sinking her they extracted from her crew valuable information regarding the convoy's intentions, even to the eventual rendezvous should the convoy be scattered by weather or attack.

After sinking the ship the destroyers tore along the convoy route, emerged from a snow-squall to find that they had caught up with the tail-end of the re-forming convoy. And the cruiser *Trinidad* and two British destroyers *Fury* and *Eclipse*! *Fury* in particular was a well-blooded veteran. She had been on this frozen run before. A glimpse of the German destroyers was enough. Joyfully both *Fury* and *Eclipse* hurled themselves at the intruders under conditions that must have been terrifying. There were snow-squalls, and as the destroyers tore through the angry water at more than thirty knots, the spray enveloped them and froze as it fell. *Fury* and *Eclipse* caught the German destroyer Z26 in an ideal position and promptly sank her.

The other two German destroyers, firmly convinced that a cruiser and two fighting-mad destroyers was a different kettle of fish from the tail-end of a bewildered convoy, withdrew hurriedly—doubtless to return home to relate a story of having fought at least half the British destroyer force in northern waters. . . . Sad to relate, *Trinidad* was hit by a torpedo. She finally limped into Kola Inlet and subsequent examination of the debris in her revealed the astonishing fact that one of her own torpedoes had run wild, circled and hit her!

In the meantime PQ13 was having a running fight against U-boats. A ship was torpedoed and disabled; another ship, the *Induna,* courageously took her in tow and slowly heaved her along at four knots. Such courage deserved a better fate, but *Induna* and her tow were both sunk, as was another ship. The crew of *Induna* managed to get away in their life-boats and had to endure the torture of three days and nights in indescribable conditions before they were picked up by one of the fleet sweepers which had sailed from Kola to escort the ships in the last stages of their run.

The sweepers, ships of the 6th Minesweeping Flotilla based on Kola, left harbour as the first trickles of information came in of the running fight against U-boats and destroyers around PQ13. *Harrier, Gossamer, Speedwell* and *Hussar* had only scanty details, but they knew that *Harpalion* had been bombed but was still afloat and fighting back, that about 180 miles north of her *Empire Ranger* was sinking rapidly, that *Induna* had been torpedoed and a U-boat was attacking the merchant ship *Effingham* with every chance of success. The rest of the convoy was scattered, as were also the escorts after their fights with German destroyers and U-boats.

Commander A. D. H. Jay, the Senior Officer of the flotilla, in *Harrier,* sent *Speedwell* off to search for survivors while he led the other two, *Gossamer* and *Hussar,* along the convoy route in the hope of rounding up the scattered ships. A gloomy prospect faced Lieutenant-Commander T. E. Williams in *Speedwell.* She plunged on into the heavy seas knowing only that somewhere in the savage murk were cockleshell lifeboats and rafts with men in them, clinging desperately to the slender shreds of life and hope. Also, so far as he knew, there were at least three German destroyers out there, each far more heavily armed than was his own ship. *Speedwell* plunged on alone.

To Commander Jay came the news that *Trinidad* had been torpedoed and was limping along through snowstorms. He set off in his ship to try to find her, and in the dusk of the early afternoon he located her steaming along at four knots taking a savage beating from the tremendous seas. *Harrier* passed a wire hawser to *Trinidad* and helped the cruiser to stay stern-on to the seas until finally she reached more sheltered waters. What an epic lies concealed in these few words! But *Harrier* had not finished; she steamed off into the night and found a small Norwegian whaler converted into a minesweeper, wallowing alone—completely out of oil fuel. She also was towed to shelter by *Harrier* who, before once more setting out to rejoin *Hussar*, *Gossamer* and possibly *Speedwell*, transferred some oil fuel to the Norwegians.

The next day, in a momentary break in a blinding snowstorm, an alert look-out caught a glimpse of red, a mere speck, in the water. It was the sail of *Effingham's* lifeboat. Two officers and thirteen men had managed to get it into the water and for a night and a day they had sailed grimly on. Five men had slipped into eternal sleep in the boat when *Harrier* found them.

Finally, on 30 March—ten days after it had sailed from Reykjavik—PQ13 limped into Murmansk having lost five ships in the voyage. Aircraft had sunk two, one had been sunk by the German destroyers, and two had been torpedoed by U-boats. In a word, a quarter of the convoy had been lost on a run of ten days, during which four and a half had been so weather-scourged that nothing could operate against them.

While Admiral Tovey fought for more small ships for escorts, more destroyers, more corvettes and more trawlers for the precious convoys, he also fought as strenuously for the number of convoys to be reduced during the following months. With longer hours of daylight approaching, the Germans would be increasingly favoured, for they were by now building up a formidable force of U-boats, aircraft and heavy surface craft in north Norway. At the same time Admiral Dudley Pound, the First Sea Lord, forcibly pointed out to the Defence Committee that, under the conditions which would prevail during the next six or seven months, running convoys would inevitably involve heavy losses in merchant ships and warships. But political pressure was too great for them. Presumably some expert advised the Defence Committee that unless the convoys were continued —and in larger strength, too—the Russians might feel neglected and would sue for a separate peace! Roosevelt and Churchill, while recognizing the inevitability of heavy losses, pressed hard for the convoys to continue.

Weight of German air and under-water attack were not the only concern of the naval ships. The escorts all along had laboured under the extreme disadvantage that they were not adequately equipped to deal with any heavy air attack. Apart from the newer fleet destroyers, their anti-aircraft armament was pitiable. Many of the destroyers of older vintage had lost some of their guns so that they could ship larger quantities of depth-charges. The 4-inch guns which were fitted to the destroyers and, for that matter, to the fleet sweepers, corvettes and trawlers, could not be elevated high enough to shoot at dive-bombers—a hard lesson learned in Norway and Dunkirk. Their anti-aircraft armament consisted of two-pounder pom-poms and .5-inch machine-guns, and for the trawlers and corvettes a brace of Lewis guns. Later came the long-barrelled 20-millimetre Oerlikon and other refinements, but the early escorts were indeed badly armed against aircraft.

The Russians, too, were singularly unco-operative, even in the early stages. They flatly declined to use their anti-submarine ships around Kola Inlet and the eastern part of the Barents Sea where the U-boats were congregating, neither would they provide fighter escort to offset the German air attack from adjacent Petsamo. When confronted with our mounting losses in warships and merchant ships, their only reaction was 'Send more ships, use more escorts!'

So PQ14 was planned, many of the ships being American Liberty ships or tankers which had steamed across the Atlantic in submarine-hammered convoys, and it sailed on 8 April, twenty-four ships strong, with a powerful escort and the inevitable cruiser-and-destroyer screening force. It was sailed north of previous routes because the ice was receding—or it was assumed that it would be. Shortly after leaving Iceland the convoy ran into pack-ice, more alarming in looks than in actual fact, but a lot of the ships' masters had never met pack-ice before, and sixteen of them turned back to Iceland. Eight sailed on and one was sunk by a U-boat, a solitary submarine on patrol which escaped by diving under the heavy ice-floes.

By now events had begun to assume a definite pattern. The Germans were maintaining extensive submarine patrols off Iceland in order to report the ships which came under sailing orders, and to hang on to the convoy, attacking it wherever possible, but always reporting the progress of the convoy—speed, course and disposition of the escort. Once these factors were established, the Germans could launch an air attack and increase the force of submarines to assault the convoy. Further, if conditions were suitable, they could send out a heavy surface raiding force which always had the bolt-hole back to Norway should things become too hot.

Four

SHIPS lying empty at Murmansk or Kola were a dead loss. The Russians had nothing to offer for return cargoes, so the ships had to sail back in ballast. At any time, and in any sea, a voyage in ballast with ships high out of the water, wallowing all over the show, is far from pleasant, and in those merciless northern waters sailing in convoy in ballast was sheer hell. No two ships react alike to bad weather: one, for instance, will plunge headlong into a mountainous, creamtopped sea, hesitate on the crest and, with scarcely any warning, will swing away almost at right angles. With room to move and no other ships in the vicinity, a ship's master can cope with this situation; he would know his vessel's best point for lying hove-to, would reduce speed and let her ride it out. With a number of ships in convoy, all sheering about at different angles like startled cattle and in darkness, it was a nightmare of nightmares. The frothing top of every wave became, in the blackness, the bow wave of another ship. And it went on for endless hours while the gales raged.

Add to this situation vicious and prolonged snowstorms which shut down visibility to a few yards, plus the possibility —even the probability—of some U-boats and raiding destroyers, then one begins to wonder how in Heaven's name those who sailed in the Arctic convoys retained their reason. It was such a prospect which faced convoy QP10 formed at Kola to make the run to Iceland. Sixteen ships strong, it sailed early in April 1942. Its escort was five destroyers: *Oribi*, *Punjabis*, *Marne*, *Fury* and patched-up *Eclipse*. There were also the weary and battered minesweeper *Speedwell* returning for a long-overdue refit, as well as two trawlers, *Blackfly* and *Paynter*.

On paper this seems a reasonably strong escort and one capable of looking after an Atlantic convoy where the main threat would be submarines and possibly a surface raider. To meet this last contingency the cruiser *Liverpool* was in the wings, to join the convoy at close quarters during the day to provide anti-aircraft support, and to stand away at twilight and darkness. But Commander J. E. H. McBeath, in *Oribi*, the senior ship, knew that of his five destroyers only *Marne* had any weight of anti-aircraft armament. The others were equipped with one single 3-inch or 4-inch high-angle gun and a few pom-poms. The Germans arrogantly put up an observation plane from their airfield forty or fifty miles away and watched the convoy form. There was no attempt by the Russians either to drive it away or shoot it down.

So QP10 sailed. At first light next morning German aircraft attacked and met with an unpleasant surprise. The convoy was waiting for them, and two JU88s were rapidly tumbled into the water, and two or three more reeled away damaged. One JU88 wriggled and twisted its way through the tracer and shell-pitted sky and scored a hit on the ship *Empire Cowper*. Her crew was taken off and she sank, but the convoy retained formation. Then came a prolonged and welcome snowstorm which blinded the aircraft, whilst the ships, heavily coated in frozen snow and spray, resembled the icebergs which occasionally loomed up in the grey light.

One lone aircraft in a brief lull did however slip through *Punjabi's* fire, set its bomb-sights on a ship, missed her and shattered a small ice-floe. *Punjabi's* gunner decided to award him a coconut, if they could find one growing in Iceland!

But now the main threats were U-boats which were known to be lying in wait. Unfortunately the cold layers of water cut down the efficiency of the asdic sets and one U-boat slipped through the vigilant screen and in the darkness torpedoed *Kiev*. An escort was detached to pick up her crew, and then less than an hour later another torpedo thudded into *El Occidente's* flanks and she, too, required an escort to take off her crew. *Oribi* made contact with a U-boat and framed her in depth-charges with unknown results, except that there were no more submarine raids on the convoy.

Grey daylight arrived with much too much visibility and two sharp raids by JU88s. The second raid cost the Germans four aircraft, but they succeeded in sinking *Harpalion*, the ship which had been bombed and damaged in PQ13, but had been rescued by the sweepers of the 6th Flotilla. Then came prolonged and blessed fog. The convoy altered course, slipped through the writhing grey mass and the Germans never succeeded in finding it again. A few days of hard weather and the convoy wearily anchored at Reykjavik, having lost four ships (a quarter of its total)—two to bombers and two to U-boats.

The pattern had been maintained through the long winter months of almost endless night: darkness, fog, slamming gales were allies and, providing a convoy was resolutely handled, it could escape extreme heavy punishment. Another pattern also began to take definite shape. Admiral Tovey and the admirals under him and, for that matter, all the commanding officers of the ships which had to escort and screen the convoys—from rear-admirals down to the lieutenants who commanded the small ships in the wearisome convoys—knew that as the daylight hours increased so also would the weight of the onslaught upon them be intensified. They knew that sooner or later there would be a full-sized disaster with a convoy completely destroyed—quite possibly with half or more of the escorting ships sunk. And they were under no illusions about where the blame would fall, regardless of where it was merited.

The pressure was maintained. The Beaverbrook Mission had made the promises; it was up to the Navy and the merchant ships—most of them American—to fulfil those promises. Roosevelt pressed Churchill, Churchill pressed the Admiralty, the Admiralty pressed Admiral Tovey, and sundry small ships and freighters once more wearily hove up their anchors, steamed into position and . . . another convoy was on its way. It was just like that.

So at the end of April, when any Hull or Grimsby trawler skipper could have told the insistent planners that the nights off Bear Island were growing shorter and the days were oh, so long, yet another convoy was formed and under way. Convoy PQ15 sailed from Iceland on 26 April, an ominously fine morning with just a touch of tartness in the spring air.

It was twenty-five ships strong with a redoubtable escort. Captain J. H. F. Crombie, as Senior Officer in the minesweeper *Bramble*, had with him his group of four sweepers going back to Russia for a turn of duty there, six destroyers, including *Somali*, *Matchless* and a Hunt-class which were well-armed with high-angle anti-aircraft guns, four pugnacious trawlers, and a specially equipped anti-aircraft ship, *Ulster Queen*. An escort of fifteen ships for a convoy of twenty-five! The Commodore was Captain H. J. Anchor, RNR, in *Botavon*.

PQ15 steamed steadily north in the conventional convoy columns without being molested, but with the knowledge that the inevitable shadowing submarine was about. The course and timing were set so that the convoy would meet and pass QP11 somewhere off Bear Island, weather and Germans permitting.

Also at sea, alert and ready for another foray by *Tirpitz* or a sister ship, was Admiral Tovey with a heavy force of combined British and American battleships and attendant destroyer screen, and the cruisers *Nigeria* and *London*. QP11 had an awe-inspiring escort and screening force when compared with the escorts which were battling convoys across the Atlantic. The weight reflected the Royal Navy's determination that, so far as it was concerned, it would have to be acknowledged that it was doing its damnedest. Covering QP11 when it sailed from Russia was the cruiser *Edinburgh*, carrying the flag of Rear-Admiral Bonham-Carter, an escort of six destroyers, four corvettes and two trawlers. In addition, too, the convoy was escorted some of the way by the British minesweepers based on Russia as well as four Russian destroyers.

On 29 April enemy aircraft and U-boats reported convoy QP11. The submarines hung on to the skirts of the convoy while other submarines were gathering themselves in force astride the course of the convoy (incidentally, across the course of PQ15, too) while the aircraft circled and waited. *Edinburgh* was torpedoed the following day, as she steamed ahead and across the track of the convoy, by one of the shadowing submarines, U-456. A handsome dividend for a submarine which was in reality merely shadowing. *Edinburgh* turned about and started to limp back to Murmansk with two watchful destroyers circling her, which meant that the escorting force was minus two valuable destroyers.

On 1 May—the next day—the weakened escort of QP11 fought off a sharp attack by U-boats without loss to the convoy. This was followed shortly afterwards by an attack by Heinkel 111s which were met by a savage barrage and driven off without any vessels, escort or merchant ship, suffering more than superficial damage.

The submarine shadowing the convoy had reported *Edinburgh's* damage and the emboldened Germans sent three destroyers racing to sea from Altenfiord to collect what dividend they could. They elected to tackle the convoy first. In the initial fight the destroyer *Amazon* was damaged, leaving three British destroyers with their 4-inch guns to fight off the raiders armed with 5-inch. The Senior Officer of the destroyers, Commander M. Richmond in *Bulldog*, reflected in his own personality and in the name of his ship the tenacity of the remaining three ships. Throughout the afternoon of the May Day, Commander Richmond and his two consorts kept up a running fight against the German destroyers—never forgetting for a moment that his primary task was to prevent the Germans from getting among the merchant ships. While the Germans could manœuvre and speed away to attack at any angle they chose, Richmond had to be certain that he and his hard-pressed ships were always between the convoy and the attackers. And he succeeded—outweighted, outgunned, he was never out-manœuvred. At long last the German destroyers turned away. Those grim, smoke-begrimed, deafened men on the three British destroyers, knee-deep in empty shell-cases, must have watched the Germans wheel away for the last time with considerable relief.

Inside their screen of ships the convoy still sailed on, almost sedately, ship following ship, keeping station as if they were supremely confident that those three snarling, fire-spitting destroyers would not let through the heavier German craft. And their confidence was not misplaced. Even the sweaty faces on *Bulldog* cracked into a tired grin when one destroyer signalled her: 'I would not like to play poker against you with you holding three of a kind.' It had indeed been a game of bluff with the stake increased to the limit when necessary.

The German destroyers tore off eastward in search of *Edinburgh*, and found her. Around her circled two British destroyers which the Germans treated with marked respect, preferring to fight them at extreme range, a salutary lesson taught them by *Bulldog* and her consorts being still painfully fresh in their minds. *Edinburgh* though a cripple was by no means helpless, and thundered back at the destroyers attacking her. But the destroyer *Forester* reeled away from repeated hits, slowed down and eventually lay rolling on the uneasy sea.

Edinburgh hit and disabled the German destroyer *Hermann Schoemann* which the *Forester*, immobile but not stingless, as well as the destroyer *Foresight*, continued to hammer until *Foresight* in turn was heavily hit. The German destroyers closed in, torpedoed *Edinburgh* once more, almost cutting her in half. A delectable dish was thus laid out for the remaining German destroyers—a cruiser and two British destroyers lying more or less helpless.

The British ships waited for the kill which seemed almost inevitable, but to their intense amazement the Germans did not close in. One of them made a rapid dash in to rescue the survivors of the *Hermann Schoemann*, then tore off westward and disappeared. The explanation for this unexpected behaviour is almost comically simple. Steaming to escort the stricken *Edinburgh* back to Murmansk came four British fleet sweepers, part of the force based in north Russia. As they steamed through the haze in line ahead the Germans imagined that they were four more destroyers hastening to join in the fight. Obviously suffering from a surfeit of British destroyers, they decided to call it a day and sheered off home. Eventually *Forester* and *Foresight* managed to carry out repairs enough for them to limp on; but before they did so they had one sorrowful task to perform. The smitten *Edinburgh* was finally finished off with British torpedoes.

And QP11, the cause of all the fighting, reached home

without any further trouble. It passed PQ15 the next day, and between the attenuated escort of QP11 and the powerful ships guarding PQ15, there passed some gloomy signals laden with prophecies of troubles to come.

Five

THE prophets were not false. In the half-light of early morning on 3 May, torpedo-bombers swept in low over the sea and attacked PQ15. When they wheeled away, framed in the vicious tracer and smoke bursts of the barrage, they left behind them three ships sinking.

They sank the Commodore ship, *Botavon*, and the *Jutland*, and the crews were taken off. *Cape Corso*, loaded deeply with ammunition, was also hit, but there was no rescue—there was one furious breath-taking explosion, a seething rose-coloured column of flame and in a few seconds only fragments descending to the water remained.

If ever gunners added a little more of that something into their shooting, they did so within the next hour. One attack of twelve torpedo-bombers—a new introduction by the Germans, incidentally—had four blasted out of the sky without their reaching a ship. But scarcely had they disappeared when the U-boats attacked, and the escorts made the sea boil and erupt as they carried out counter-attack after counter-attack. There was no time to push the attacks farther: 'Keep the subs down and the convoy moving' was the watchword. And they did. Throughout that long morning, escorts broke away from the screen around the convoy as alert asdic ratings reported firm contacts, and no submarine got through to torpedo a ship. And in the afternoon came relief. The weather broke, snow-squalls, visibility down to a couple of hundred yards, less at times, defeated the attempts to inflict another air attack. Furthermore, the submarines, driven away to their limits, were forced to remain submerged and so failed to detect any change of course carried out by the Commodore. And they lost the convoy. PQ15 arrived without losing any more ships.

To sum up: thirty-eight ships in two convoys had sailed through those waters, at times quite close to one another, and had arrived with a sum total of four losses. By contemporary standards, considering the persistent weight of attack against them—aircraft, submarines and destroyers—it was a triumph for the escorting forces which were doing what they said would be extremely difficult, if not impossible, and which the planners said could be done. That is, the convoys got through. But at what a price! A price demanded of the escorting forces, a price demanded in naval ships at a time when every one was a pearl immeasurable in price. *Edinburgh* sunk; *Forester* and *Foresight* badly damaged; and, of the distant screening force, the destroyer *Punjabis* rammed and sunk by *King George V*. And that was not all. The cruiser *Trinidad*, damaged while escorting an earlier convoy, had been patched up in Russia sufficiently to make the passage home. She set out with a screen of four destroyers on 12 May. She was inevitably located and reported and the angry, frustrated German planes, still wrathful at losing the convoys, came out to attack her with torpedo-bombers and bombers. Under repeated attacks

Trinidad was again severely damaged, uncontrollable fires broke out on her, and it was decided to sink her with our own torpedoes.

When Admiral Tovey resumed his plea that convoying in summer should be discontinued until the autumn, he had at his elbow a frightening list of naval losses—the most recent being two cruisers and two destroyers. He said that if they (the convoys) must be continued for political reasons, then very serious and heavy losses must be expected. In this he was supported by the First Sea Lord who said: 'The whole thing is a most unsound operation with the dice loaded against us in every direction.'

And the answer? C-in-C Home Fleet was ordered to arrange escort for convoy PQ16—largest convoy yet formed for Russia. Thirty-eight ships—a convoy to sail against an enemy alerted to the increasing supplies being ferried to Russia, a convoy which would have to run the gauntlet in almost continuous daylight. To sail the other way—homeward-bound—was QP12 comprising fifteen ships. And there was now an added threat: the *Scheer* was known to have joined up with *Lützow* at Narvik with attendant destroyers. A formidable force was thus poised only a few hours' steaming-time from the area where these two convoys would pass. There would be fifty-three merchant ships in those one-time deserted, bleak waters, two convoys almost impacted into one mass of shipping. It was essential, to meet this threat, that the Home Fleet should be somewhere in the wings with a cruiser force and strong destroyer screen not far away from the convoys.

So PQ16 sailed on 16th May, and QP12 on the same day.

The close escort for the convoys was large enough to have escorted three or four Atlantic convoys, or at least was as large as the escorts covering three or four Atlantic convoys, a subtle difference. A covering screen was arranged of not one cruiser or two, but four. There were *Nigeria*, *Norfolk*, *Kent* and *Liverpool*, with attendant destroyers. If German surface forces did sail to attack before they could do so, they would have a fight on their hands. But how great a sacrifice would the gods demand?

The cruisers and destroyers positioned themselves to the east to cover the first part of QP12's passage, and maintained that position until the two convoys were passing one another, never far away yet never too close to be hampered in the case of an attack by the German heavy ships. The Germans had airily given up sending out spotting planes to search for convoys, for they knew that ultimately the convoys would have to pass east and west, either north or south of Bear Island, depending on how far down the ice had come. So why waste time searching the broad expanses when, aided by U-boat reports, they could locate a convoy in a couple or three hours? In those northern latitudes at that time of the year the sky is a brilliant blue, almost a deep indigo towards evening, and the sea is like a sheet of polished metal. In such a setting it was impossible to hide fifty-odd ships and their escorts.

The first shadowing plane appeared on the afternoon of the 25th as the two convoys, PQ16 and QP12, were approaching one another, so the plane had in sight a target of more than a hundred ships including the close escorts. This was the sort of thing that the Luftwaffe had been waiting for. The German aircraft concentrated on PQ16, and an air-battle began which continued throughout the remainder of the trip. Heinkel 111s and JU88s hammered at the convoy with torpedoes and bombs. The CAM (Catapult Aircraft Merchant) ship *Empiré Lawrence* was torpedoed, but not before her single Hurricane was sent off and had shot down one Heinkel and sent another reeling away smoking furiously.

The CAM ships deserve a short description or, rather, the pilots of their solitary planes do. On the foredeck of a CAM ship was erected a powerful catapult which could launch a Hurricane fighter. The plane would roar into the air, be engaged in combat until its ammunition was expended, and then the pilot would parachute into the sea, as close to rescue or escort ship as possible, and wait until picked up—a most unenviable job. To begin with, the Hurricanes allocated for this job, as they were completely expendable once launched, were not in the best of health. All that was asked of them was a swift attack before the pilot baled out. Furthermore, it is a moot point as to how valuable they would be in a fight against fifty or sixty enemy aircraft.

Sometimes, with convoys expecting to do a sharp turn away from course, the Hurricane could be launched against the Snooping Joe shadower and the ships would be treated to the brief spectacle of the shadower fleeing across the sky pursued by a determined fighter, with, occasionally, success being marked by a downwards trailing thin line of smoke. Baling out of a Hurricane into those Arctic waters in summer-time was far from pleasant—the water being just about at freezing-point and a sharp rescue vital.

In winter-time, if the rescuing ship was at all dilatory—even muffing the pick-up by five minutes—then it picked up a stiffening youngster who had joined the ever-increasing ranks of those who had given without counting the cost. . . . Arctic waters in winter-time are merciless killers.

The air attacks continued at frequent intervals through the unending light night and all through 26 May. When the aircraft were not swooping in, the U-boats made sporadic attacks but achieved no more success than the aircraft. On the 27th the four cruisers left the convoy. Let us not lose sight of their primary task which was to be between the convoy and any surface craft which sallied forth from Norway.

And the air attacks increased in severity. Like gnats dancing in the summer heavens, the aircraft could be seen against the ice-blue sky, at first giving no impression of speed. The higher layers of bombers came first, growing larger in the gun-sights. Their bombs dropped, they swung away and low over the water, so low some of them that their slip-stream ruffled and darkened the surface. Next came the torpedo-bombers—twisting, weaving, threading their way through a sky filled with the small clouds of smoke from shell-bursts and the deadly lacework of tracer-bullets. Some failed to face up to the intense barrage at the vital point in their run and swung off to live and attack another day. Others, whose courage cannot be doubted, thrust their attacks home . . . and a few of them hit the sea in a brief column of spray. In all, 108 air attacks were logged by one of the escort ships. In a momentary lull the losses were assessed.

Astern of the convoy were two ships lying motionless, one still in flames, both sinking. Moving slowly from the path of the convoy disabled, also ultimately to go under, were two more. Four ships sunk and an escort—the Polish destroyer *Garland,* a redoubtable and renowned fighter, asking no quarter and certainly giving none—was damaged, but not out of action. At midnight, marked only by the passage of time but with no diminution in the light, a fresh series of air attacks swept in and two more ships were sunk.

The Commodore ship *Ocean Voice* was badly holed and set on fire. With choking clouds of smoke rolling over her and water pouring through the gaping wound, her DEMS gunners, oftentimes blinded by the smoke, slammed back with some success at the aircraft which concentrated their venom on her. Whilst the guns thudded and chattered, *Ocean Voice's* crew fought the fire and struggled to minimize the severity of the damage. Such courage was not unrewarded. When the remnants of the convoy steamed in, *Ocean Voice,* battered, charred, and with water feet deep in her, was still leading, still Commodore ship.

On the 28th, during a fresh outburst of air attacks, yet another ship was sunk. By this time, though, the gunners on the merchant ships and escorts were wearied beyond telling: they were automatons—loading, firing, shifting target, firing and loading by sheer instinct, each move an exaggerated gesture, as they fought against the overwhelming weariness. They moved, and looked, like sleep-walkers. Then the air attacks petered out. The convoy limped on, scarcely daring to believe that there were no planes in the sky, no skimming torpedo-planes, no bombing planes. Just clear, blue sky. On the 29th there was a brief flurry as a solitary enemy plane threaded its way high over the convoy. And that was all.

The fire on *Ocean Voice*, not completely subdued, broke out afresh and the fight started once more. Not far behind her, still steaming in her position in the convoy, was another ship, a Russian, the *Stori*, and she, too, trailed behind her a darkening cloud of smoke as fire strove to gain a hold on her cargo.

On 30 May six ships appeared, pin-pointed on the razor-sharp line between water and sky. From the funnels of escorts came brief puffs of smoke as the ships increased speed to insert themselves between the newcomers and the convoy. White lights twinkled, challenges were made and were replied to. The new arrivals were six British mine-sweepers from Murmansk to escort the battered convoy over the last few miles, and to assure that at this last stage of the journey no mine claimed a victim. Of the remaining ships left, six proceeded to Murmansk. The rest turned to-wards Kola Inlet.

Cables rattled dully through hawse-pipes, wearied hands rang 'finished with engines', men got their heads down for that most wonderful thing, sleep. Then the air-raid warning sounded over Kola Inlet; but it was brief—probably only a photographic mission.

When the shooting and the tumult had died away then came the tragic reckoning. Seven ships were lost from PQ16, two were badly damaged and yet another escort vessel damaged. Viewed against the number of ships which sailed through those waters in the two convoys, the losses were not enormous; but the sustained intensity of the German air attack over three and a half days showed that convoys passing through those waters were vulnerable for twenty-four hours of each and every day.

If the German naval chiefs had taken their courage in both hands and abandoned just for once the severe caution imposed upon them, and had mounted a triple or even quadruple attack on a convoy—by air, U-boat, destroyer and two heavy ships—a convoy could have been destroyed. There would have been, too, the possibility that we might lose two, three, or even four cruisers before the Home Fleet could bring the enemy to bay on the surface—assuming, that is, that we could catch it.

It was a nightmare of a possibility which was thrust once again before the Admiralty, and in turn before the Defence Committee, and in turn again before the people who looked at the problem from a purely political point of view. And the answer which came back down the line?

Yet another convoy. PQ17.

Six

PQ17. A convoy of thirty-six merchant ships, mostly American-built Liberty ships and tankers. Just another convoy committed to fighting its way northwards and eastwards to Russia. Many of the merchant ships were making their third, and even fourth, trips. When the curtain went up, somewhere off Bear Island, they knew that bellowing guns and snarling tracer would herald 'Beginners, please!' It would be the overture to endless long hours of fighting, of noise, of near-misses shaking the ships to their keels, of weaving aircraft. They knew that ships would be sunk, and men would die. Other ships, other men, but not themselves —such is the instinctive optimism of man.

Thirty-six fat, heavily laden merchant ships, and guarding them in close escort, or in a covering screen, or steaming between them and the German bases, were forty-six ships flying the White Ensign or the Stars and Stripes. And the ships were manned by veteran fighters, men who would not be turned aside by weight of foe or armament.

PQ17—just another convoy; but one which ultimately was to end in tragedy, a convoy which for three years was to cast an undeserved slur on the Royal Navy, a slur which had to be borne in silence against a rising tide of criticism, of scornful laughter from one end of the world to the other. . . . PQ17 sailed from Iceland on 29 June. Many of the ships had already battled across the Atlantic in Western Ocean convoys to start anew another voyage into the far north. The convoy was given a close escort of six destroyers, four corvettes, two submarines, two anti-aircraft ships, three minesweepers, four asdic trawlers. Screening it was a cruiser force comprising *London* (the ship which had carried the Beaverbrook-Harriman Mission to and from Russia at the beginning of it all), *Norfolk*, the American cruiser *Tuscaloosa* and three destroyers.

To patrol south and west of the convoy route, watchful and waiting for German surface craft to sally forth, steamed the battleship *Duke of York*, flagship of C-in-C Home Fleet, USS *Washington*, aircraft-carrier *Victorious*, and the cruisers *Nigeria* and *Cumberland* with a screen of fourteen destroyers. Forty-six fighting ships dedicated to the primary task of seeing that convoy PQ17 got through with a minimum of loss. This orderly array of ships, under Commodore J. C. K. Dowding, RNR, in *River Afton*, steamed north and easterly, settling down quite nicely.

In the afternoon of 30 June a black pin-point appeared in the sky to the south, circling the convoy at long range. And fog closed in on the convoy. Above it the ships could hear the plane, and as the fog thinned to mist they could see it occasionally. The inevitable snooper had appeared. It was a Blohm Voss 138, with its characteristic drooping nose as if it were sniffing at the convoy. Everybody knew of course what was taking place. The plane was reporting the course, speed and size of the convoy. The formula was a familiar one:

some time in the near future, maybe only hours, maybe a day or two, the sky would be filled with darting, snarling aircraft, some flying high and bombing, others just skimming the water to launch their torpedoes.

Towards evening—in time only, because there was no dusk—the fog closed down once more and through it crept the convoy. The eerie, cloaked, silence was broken only by the sound of the water rolling away from the stems of the ships and an occasional warning blast from a ship's siren. One or two of the vessels, with a good head of steam, suddenly lifted their safety-valves in a roar, to be snarled at as jumpy nerves reacted. Each ship sailed in a little white world of its own, remote, yet closely in touch with other ships. And so Flaming June passed into July.

The convoy was routed on a course as far north as was possible. It was to sail close to Jan Mayen Island, north and easterly, until it was just south of Hope Island, leaving Bear Island to its south, and then dead east until it turned south eventually for the White Sea. As it was the height of summer the ice had receded, and on its given course the convoy would skirt the edge of it. This was a mixed blessing: it would mean probably encountering a succession of fogs caused by the proximity of the ice, an added burden for this mass of shipping; but on the other hand, fog made it difficult for aircraft to shadow the convoy, almost impossible for surface craft to locate it, and every hour spent in the swirling white menace was another hour nearer Russia—and safety. Furthermore, the escorts and screening ships were certain of one thing: an attack by surface ships would be highly unlikely to develop from north of them.

The close escort was not unduly worried when the snooping plane arrived and started reporting the convoy. This force included some hardy veterans of convoy work who had had experience in the Atlantic, the fire-riven Malta convoys and earlier trips to Russia. Among them were such ships as the destroyers *Fury*, *Leamington* and *Offa*, the USS destroyer *Wainwright* with the famous 'Jackie' Broome as Senior Officer in *Keppel*. In addition to being a destroyer captain of a high order, 'Jackie' Broome was famous throughout the Navy for some brilliant cartoons. In that field he was the equal of the top-flight men whose works grace nationally known pages.

His cartoons were used to illustrate the pages of *Western Approaches Convoy Instructions*, and besides pointing a moral pushed the point well home with an ironic twist which could not be missed. One, I recall, with now mellowing thoughts, is of three or four dejected men sitting in a carley float with the convoy disappearing over the horizon. It bore the caption: 'Extraordinary Meeting of the Stragglers Club'. I remember it because my almost inevitable job—until promotion lifted me from it—was cajoling, bullying, pleading, threatening and almost ramming some recalcitrant ship in its invariable position at dawn five miles astern of the convoy and making more smoke than a Sheffield steel-works because the skipper had told a little white lie—involving an astounding optimistic estimate of his ship's speed.

Included in the escort were some other redoubtable ships. They were not destroyers, but ships to be reckoned with so far as submarines and aircraft were concerned. They were the fleet minesweepers *Salamander*, *Halycon* and *Britomart*, the Atlantic-hardened corvettes *Lotus, La Malouine* and *Poppy*, and the tough asdic trawlers *Ayrshire, Lord Middleton, Lord Austin* and *Northern Gem.* All had been long tested in the fire of tribulation and had emerged true in temper. So from *Keppel* to *Northern Gem* inclusive, the appearance of the circling snooper caused no panic.

Sailing with them, too, were two anti-aircraft cruisers, converted merchant ships, *Palomares* and *Pozarica.* Aboard the latter, as war correspondent, was Godfrey Winn who had the extreme mortification of having the best story of his life resolutely suppressed by the Admiralty until some time after the war ended, when he finally (and, I suspect, a little defiantly) published it under the title PQ17. Winn returned from Russia to serve as a rating on the Arctic veteran cruiser *Cumberland*, refusing a commission, and lived a mess-deck life with his heartrending story locked safely in his bosom.

The 2nd of July found the convoy steaming along on a polished brass sea with a blue dome above, visibility being infinity. As it steamed along on a sea and beneath a sky which made war seem a million miles away, the Senior Officers of the escorts and the Commodore on the SS *River Afton* received a signal from the Senior Naval Officer in Russia that their destination, Murmansk, was going up in flames—a third of it had already been destroyed. The Germans, raiding from Kirkenes and Petsamo, had decided that if they could not prevent most of the ships in convoys from arriving, then they would see to it that there was nowhere left for them to arrive at. So Murmansk was burning. War was not so many miles away after all. . . .

The next day the Germans made their first attack with

half a dozen Heinkel torpedo-carrying planes. Before the planes could get near the convoy, *Fury* blasted one out of the sky and the others turned away from the concentrated barrage. But nobody had any delusions. It was merely a plucking of the strings, a few tentative breathings into instruments. The orchestra was yet to strike up in unison. Before it could do so, though, there came a signal from the Admiralty that the German surface ships *Tirpitz, Hipper* and four destroyers had left Trondhjem.

A decoy convoy had dragged its skirts across the path of the German ships, hoping to pull them near the Home Fleet and US battleships and accompanying cruisers. But in that same fog which had shrouded PQ17, *Tirpitz* and *Hipper* had missed the decoy convoy, and were out somewhere in the sea between North Cape and PQ17. This was disturbing news, but *Tirpitz* had raided north before, and had narrowly escaped discovery and possible destruction by the Home Fleet. Somewhere in the vicinity were *Duke of York, Washington* and the aircraft-carrier *Victorious*, the cruisers and more than a dozen destroyers. This time might be more conclusive.

PQ17 plodded on. No other attack developed, although in these very same waters, close to Bear Island, the previous convoy PQ16 had been incessantly attacked hour after hour, day after day. To the north of the ships, icebergs made a frieze of translucent colour—vivid greens, indigo blues and rich purples with flashing white bases as the seas broke against them.

But there were no aircraft, no submarines, no surface craft. The strain by now was beginning to tell. Although the sun shone endlessly, it was cold, exhaustingly cold, and the men had to be at the ready—without any let-up—for the submarines they knew were somewhere out there and for the aircraft which could appear in the twinkling of an eye. They had to be on tiptoe, too, for the sudden, heart-stopping bulk of German battleships.

4 July. A date of significance to the American ships in the convoy. The day was only a couple of hours old when a Heinkel bomber dropped out of the sky, skimmed the water, and gained its first victim. The *Christopher Newport* reeled away from the convoy, engines stopped, heavy smoke rolling from her in clouds. She was finally sunk by a torpedo from one of our own submarines accompanying the convoy, M614, because, badly damaged as she was, she might have floated for a while, a danger to any following ships.

The next attack carried weight and resolution. Twenty-five Heinkels swept in at masthead height, hitting the convoy on the starboard quarter. The sky was criss-crossed with flaming tracer and heavily pock-marked with the little blobs of smoke from shells. Some of the German planes faltered, slipped over on one wing and tumbled into the water, but others continued into and over the convoy, defying the barrage. With the predatory instinct of hawks, some of the machines made for the oil tanker *Aldersdale*, from which escorts hoped to get supplies as opportunity offered. Suddenly there was a sheet of vivid flame which shot up like a golden-red column, turning to a huge mushroom of thick black smoke. The surviving Heinkels wheeled away to disappear like gnats against the sky.

Behind them they left, wallowing low in the water and

smoke pouring from them, the Russian ship *Azerbaijan* and the *William Hooper*. Four ships gone in two attacks and six enemy aircraft shot down. But there was a pleasing splash of courage about the Russian ship. Her crew had abandoned her, but when the pall of smoke mysteriously died away they boarded her once more and, limping along well behind the convoy, she finally reached her native land.

Then came a signal from the Admiralty, a part of which read: 'A move by enemy heavy units to the north is in progress. This threatens the convoy, but there is no indication of immediate danger. . . .' PQ17 had all the danger it wanted right on the spot from submarines (which had not yet taken a hand) and from aircraft. Heavy surface units would be the problem for the Home Fleet and Cruiser Force 1. Nevertheless, anxious eyes scanned the horizon for the first tell-tale bulk of the *Tirpitz* or one of the others. Neither the convoy Commodore nor the Senior Officers of the escort were unduly worried by either the signal or the vague threat of an attack by the German heavy ships. The very presence of a German 'fleet in being' in north Norway had always been a threat to convoys. For that same reason C-in-C Home Fleet had sent a covering force of cruisers and had taken his heavy ships to sea to meet any contingency which might arise in that direction.

PQ17 had lost four ships—four out of thirty-six, a ninth of the total. By contemporary measurements the convoy was doing extremely well. Around 1800 hours Admiral Hamilton, commanding Cruiser Force 1, confident that PQ17 and its escort were quite happy, signalled to the Admiralty and C-in-C Home Fleet that his intention was to leave it at 2200 hours. Then began a series of ambiguous signals from the Admiralty which merely succeeded in adding confusion to confusion, and which ultimately ended in tragedy.

At 1930 hours Admiral Hamilton received back a signal instructing him to remain with the convoy pending further orders. Part of it read: 'Further information may be available shortly.' Even this did not seriously perturb him. The Admiralty, he presumed, and rightly, would have more intelligence available than he had, and would perhaps come up later with something about the German heavy surface craft. He realized that if they were in the offing it would be his job to take the first impact, perhaps to take quite a beating until the heavy ships of the Home Fleet arrived; but it was for precisely that reason that his force had sailed. It was to protect a convoy, PQ17, from destruction. Based on experience, it was assumed that any surface attack would materialize roughly abeam of Bear Island—and it would be highly improbable, becoming even more improbable as the convoy moved east of that position. So Admiral Hamilton's instructions were to leave the convoy when it was east of twenty-five degrees east—that is, east of Bear Island—unless something turned up to make it expedient for him to remain with it.

At 2100 hours came a signal to Admiral Hamilton bearing the prefix: 'Most immediate. Cruiser Force withdraw to westward at high speed.' Following this came a second signal from the Admiralty also prefixed 'Immediate'. It read: 'Owing to threat of surface ships convoy is to disperse and proceed to Russian ports independently.' Before this second signal had been thoroughly digested by the destroyers and cruisers and the convoy Commodore—in fact, within two minutes of its receipt, there came another from the Admiralty prefixed 'Most immediate'. It read: 'Convoy is to scatter.'

Now this was the picture. Somewhere, vaguely south, were units of the German navy, heavy ships which presumably had sailed with the fixed intention of destroying PQ17. The close escorts and the Cruiser Force 1 did not know either what units there were, or where they were. But the series of signals taken in their order of receipt quite rightly led to the belief that some enemy surface craft were rapidly closing the convoy. First, Admiral Hamilton was instructed to go east of his original zero line, twenty-five degrees east. Secondly, there was the signal instructing him that he was to proceed westerly at high speed. Thirdly, the convoy was ordered to 'scatter'.

Now there is a marked difference between a convoy being ordered to 'disperse' and being ordered to 'scatter'. A convoy can be assumed to have reached a safe area, no longer be subject to sustained attack, and can disperse each ship to go about its lawful business of arriving in port to discharge its cargo. Or it can disperse to an orderly pattern to reduce risk and confuse an enemy. 'Scatter' has a distinct air of urgency about it. It means just what it says. Scatter! Scatter for your lives, or else . . . ! 'Scatter' is an order given only in a dire emergency. In fact, to only one other convoy in the history of convoying during the war was that order given, and that was when the armed merchant liner *Jervis Bay* courageously turned to meet her doom at the hands of a German raider, made smoke for the concealment of the convoy and signalled 'Scatter'. That convoy scattered like confetti on a windy wedding-day. And it lived while *Jervis Bay* died.

The purport of the signals travelled down the lines of the stolid merchant ships, through the escort ships which felt that up to now they were doing a fairly solid job of protecting the convoy. Aircraft had attacked in force and had been beaten off. There had been losses, but every convoy suffered losses. The triumph or defeat was measured in terms of ships lost. And PQ17 had lost only four ships—actually only three, for the Russian tanker had finally limped along.

Now it was to scatter! Not only was it to scatter, but the ships covering it were to steam away and leave it. They were ordered to proceed independently to Russia [*sic*], through waters thick with German submarines, through waters roofed by a cloudless sky in which darted German aircraft from whose eyes nothing was hidden. Admiral Hamilton, quite convinced that his cruisers were being turned back to meet German raiders at any moment, signalled to the destroyers accompanying the convoy that he was turning westwards immediately. Broome, as befitted a destroyer Senior Officer, turned his ships to strengthen Hamilton's force. That, as events shaped then, was the correct thing to do. It was expected that at any moment they would be bracketed by shells from the German raiders. The ships in the convoy watched their escorting destroyers turn from them. *Keppel*, and *Fury*, the hard-hitting veteran which had blasted the first of the raiding German planes out of the sky. Then *Offa*, *Leamington* and the US destroyer *Wainwright* turning to steam in the opposite way.

To the convoy it appeared that something really big was brewing, something out of the ordinary in the way of attacks. And the cruisers and destroyers were turning back to meet it, to see that the first brunt, at least, was borne before it could hit the convoy. Then Commodore Dowding, in *River Afton*, gave the signal: 'Scatter'. Many of the seamen in the merchant ships, not completely aware of what was going on, formed their own conclusions, built up their own interpretations—particularly the seamen on the American ships. And who could blame them?

They now found themselves aboard ships which less than an hour ago had been closely and heavily guarded by a redoubtable escort and were now scattering to port and starboard. . . . The stories they subsequently related are still alive, bandied from mouth to mouth, from ship to ship. I have heard them myself, told with a wealth of circumstantial evidence.

And to where was the convoy to scatter? South of them loomed the expanses of the Barents Sea well within reach of German aircraft from Kirkenes and Petsamo. North of them was the impenetrable ice; east of them, a trackless waste of unknown water with the long finger of Novaya Zemlya. Around them, skulking on the outskirts, were the U-boats, whilst at any time there could appear in the sky the German aircraft.

And PQ17 scattered.

Seven

Now let us retrace our steps a few hours to the Admiralty. There can be no doubt that because of the almost unceasing supply of information, the Admiralty was bound to be in receipt of a tremendous amount of intelligence some of which was not known to Senior Officers on the spot. The normal procedure was to forward a digest or, if considered necessary, a long and detailed analysis of such intelligence to a Senior Officer in command of an operation to which he could add what he had already gained locally. And from the ultimate result he formed his own plans.

But what happened in the case of PQ17? Something which had been happening with distressing frequency during the period that Admiral Sir Dudley Pound was First Sea Lord. There are a number of instances recorded of the Admiralty—and what happened in the name of the Admiralty was *ipso facto* in the name of First Sea Lord—going over the heads of Senior Officers and issuing orders to convoys and escorts, and heavy ships at sea, even to the point of ordering them what course to steer. Just imagine a parallel case ashore—say, in the military field. Let us take the case of the Desert War. Montgomery, up at the front, would find his forward echelons of tanks and troops following, not his orders given to conform to his battle-plan, but some orders given by General Alexander away back in Cairo—orders given without informing Montgomery. The result would be chaos. In the case of PQ17 it was just that—more, in fact, it was tragedy, because a number of ships were sunk which need not have been sent to the bottom.

So on to trace events: C-in-C Home Fleet had disposed off North Cape a fairly tight submarine screen. Inside, comparatively close to the coast, were *Sahib, Sturgeon, Unrivalled* and *Unshaken*—names to conjure with in the submarine service—the Free French *Minerva,* as well as a Russian submarine. Outside that screen were *Ursula, Tribune, Seawolf* and *Trident.* A formidable shield indeed.

That protection would remain in force from 2 July to 5 July, when it was estimated that PQ17 would be well east of Bear Island and the submarines of the screen would move easterly to conform. To reach PQ17 any German surface units would have to penetrate that double screen of submarines which would undoubtedly report them before launching an attack.

The RAF maintained a constant watch on the German ships squatting in their Norwegian fiords, flying planes from both England and from Russia. First came intelligence flashed to the Admiralty that *Tirpitz* and *Hipper* had suddenly departed from Trondhjem sometime on the 3rd. This was news of considerable import without any doubt. Every time the German heavy surface units moved from their torpedo-shrouded fiords it was a matter of importance and it was right that everybody concerned should be warned. And they were. And it was a potential threat.

But disappearing from Trondhjem, and attacking the convoy, were two different matters. To do so, *Tirpitz* and *Hipper* would have to penetrate the submarine screen unseen, almost an impossibility under the weather conditions, and would then have to steam 500 miles or so to get into position. While there was still no further news of the two German ships, reliable intelligence arrived that *Scheer* and *Lützow* were at Altenfiord, the most northern base in Norway and a favourite jumping-off ground for the Germans when they wished to stage a threat or raid a convoy.

Adding the two items together seemed to have produced at the Admiralty a picture of preparations for a very large-scale sortie indeed, one which would tax the resources at sea under *Duke of York*. In the meantime signals began arriving that PQ17 was being heavily attacked from the air with the undoubted possibility—in fact, probability—that more attacks would occur. The last intelligence on *Scheer* and *Lützow* was that they were at Altenfiord.

A point to remember, even at the expense of being accused of granting a glimpse of the obvious, is that Intelligence is not the presentation of a complete and detailed picture. Fragmentary items of news arrive, some of them contradictory, and they have to be arranged and assessed—or even rejected when viewed against other items, often on the ground of the slim reliability of the source. For instance, a secret observer at Trondhjem, or Narvik, or even Altenfiord, might collect times and movements of German ships, hasten them to a secret radio, send the items off and the news would arrive perhaps after some hours. In the meantime, aerial observation might outdate the items.

In this particular instance, fragments of news arrived; but a Catalina which should have been flying over the fiords had an accident, and by a quirk of fate there was a gap of nearly eight hours when no air observation was carried out. The picture as it eventually presented itself to the Admiralty was that *Scheer* and *Lützow* had departed for Altenfiord, and from noon on the 3rd after leaving Trondhjem there was no news of *Tirpitz* and *Hipper*. A reasonable assumption to draw from all this was that the four German heavy units were preparing to set sail—if indeed they were not already at sea. There could be but one reason for them to sail and that was an attack on PQ17 and an attempt at its destruction.

The large-scale charts at the Admiralty gave the position of the convoy, its close escort and the cruiser screen. It also knew roughly where the *Duke of York* and her heavy consorts were. From the sum of intelligence available it seemed that if an attack by German surface units materialized it would be around 0200 hours. There was, of course, a big *if* about this. It had to be assumed that the four heavy German ships had foregathered and were either sailing or preparing to sail, as a unit. First Sea Lord, Admiral Sir Dudley Pound, called a meeting of his staff in which all the *pros* and *cons* were thoroughly discussed. While the meeting was taking place, Intelligence came in confirming that at least two of the German ships, *Tirpitz* and *Scheer*, were at Altenfiord, and were at short notice for steam. In other words, they were ready to sail at the drop of a hat. Of the others, *Lützow* and *Hipper*, there was no news and in this case it could be bad news. It was possible that they were at sea, especially as there seemed to have been a switch carried out by *Scheer* and *Hipper*.

Then followed the signals to the Admiral commanding the Cruiser Force, first to proceed east of its original line, then the next signal in effect telling him to hang on to the line as more information would be following shortly. Part of that signal reads: 'A move by enemy heavy units to the north is in progress. This threatens the convoy, but there is no indication of immediate danger. Admiralty is therefore taking no action at present, but is awaiting developments.' Nobody could cavil at that. The forces concerned were being put in the picture. It was from that point that the ominous phrase 'Someone blundered' begins to show itself through the narrative, like the thin threads of dry rot beginning to appear in otherwise unsullied timber.

Duke of York, receiving these signals, quite rightly assumed that the Admiralty—and anything that came from the Admiralty was from First Sea Lord—had intelligence not available to the ships at sea. C-in-C therefore merely kept his ships watchful and waiting. At the shortest signal: 'Enemy surface craft bearing so-and-so,' he and his force could tear forward into action. In the meantime all he could do was to wait.

First the Cruiser Force under Admiral Hamilton was ordered to withdraw westward at full speed. This was tantamount to telling the cruisers that the enemy was astern of the convoy, and their job was to get between them and slam away until the Fleet under C-in-C arrived to take over. Hamilton's force was at sea to do just that job, and instructions to withdraw to the west can be interpreted in no other way. Commander Broome, realizing that his destroyers would make a welcome addition to the Cruiser Force destroyer screen, turned and followed Admiral Hamilton's ships. Nothing deters big ships more than destroyer action thrust home resolutely, and nine destroyers hell-bent for trouble with their torpedoes could either turn or delay the Germans. Or else stop one. So *Keppel* and the others turned back.

As they did so came the signals which set the seal on the impression that disaster in the shape of German heavy units was just around the corner—first: 'Convoy is to disperse and proceed to Russian ports,' then the final one: 'Convoy is to scatter.' At the Admiralty the Staff meeting, possessed of the information that two German units had sailed, apparently weighed up the two evils. At the time the meeting was taking place PQ17 had just emerged from a heavy air attack and had emerged, if somewhat scathed and bloodied with its head unbowed. These points had to be thrashed out. When a surface attack materialized, the cruisers and convoy with the escort would be overwhelmed. If, on the other hand, still with nearly 800 miles to go, the convoy was scattered and its covering force and escort dispersed, would it prove to be an easy victim, or series of victims, for U-boats and enemy aircraft?

The meeting came to the decision that the greater danger was the surface attack. And sent the vital signal: 'Scatter.'

Now for the movements of the German units which caused these signals. *Tirpitz*, *Scheer* and *Hipper* and six destroyers finally foregathered at Altenfiord on the night of the 3rd and did not sail from there *until the afternoon of the*

5th. By that time the scattered shreds of PQ17 were being massacred by U-boats and aircraft, like the fear-ridden fleeing survivors from an Indian raid on a waggon train. *Lützow*, incidentally, never appeared in the picture at all. She and two destroyers with her ran aground while leaving Narvik.

Tirpitz, *Scheer* and *Hipper* with their six destroyers were sighted by the Russian submarine patrolling close in to the Norwegian coast, around 1700 hours. They were heading north towards a convoy which no longer existed. It no longer existed as a convoy, and many of the ships no longer existed as ships: for seventeen long, tragedy-laden hours German aircraft and U-boats had been sinking ship after ship. A patrolling aircraft reported the German fleet at 1800 hours steering east towards the spot where the convoy should have been turning south towards its goal but 350-400 miles away from it. At 2030 hours the submarine *Unshaken*, which had moved east of its original patrol line on the 4th, reported the German fleet already turning.

Less than an hour afterwards *Tirpitz*, *Scheer* and *Hipper* with their destroyers were steaming home at twenty-six knots. The operation was abandoned. They had been informed that U-boats and aircraft were seeking out the scattered ships of the late convoy PQ17, and were destroying them piecemeal. To have risked the German ships at sea to sink a few scattered vessels, with the possibility of encountering the vengeful *Duke of York*, her consorts, the cruisers of Force 1 and the cloud of destroyers they could muster, would have been carrying things to the point of foolhardiness.

The reason for the operation was the destruction of PQ17. And it was being destroyed very thoroughly, without the German ships having got within 500 miles of a single ship! There were repercussions. Many of the ships in the convoy were American, and when the survivors from them ultimately reached America, where censorship was not quite so rigid, the stories related were highly inflammatory and equally highly coloured. Flat, dogmatic accusations were made, by word of mouth and in print, particularly in neutral countries, that because of the heavy air attacks the British escort ships had turned and run away. In just those words. And not until after the war was finished was anything published to contradict those words.

How much running away there was can be measured by the subsequent actions of the various escort ships, which gathered together lone ships and formed them into little convoys which they ultimately shepherded to safety. Alas, they were a tragically small number.

Admiral Hamilton, still steaming west and following the last orders he received (direct from the Admiralty, it should be noted—not from C-in-C in *Duke of York*), was after a while convinced that his force was being used to decoy the German heavy units into the guns of *Duke of York* and *Washington* and the accompanying force. Commander Broome, in *Keppel*, began to feel an increasing uneasiness. The expected surface attack had not materialized, and astern of him was the convoy, now scattered and unescorted, suffering punishment. Successive signals began coming in: 'Torpedoed in position so-and-so.' 'Am being attacked by aircraft.' Pitiable signals devoid of hope.

Broome signalled Hamilton: 'I am always ready to go back.' Here was as broad a hint as he could make, but it was not taken. Subsequently his action in joining Force 1 was upheld by Admiral Sir John Tovey.

Somebody had to walk around with the proverbial can tied to his tail, and it was knotted securely to Admiral Hamilton's. It was considered that 'his withdrawal of escorts [i.e. Commander Broome's destroyers] was an error of judgment'. This was surely a peculiar assessment in view of the fact that had not Broome decided that his ships would strengthen Hamilton's force they would have followed orders and high-tailed it independently for Russian ports as instructed in the signal which said: 'Most immediate. Convoy is to scatter.' It was Broome, acting on his own initiative, who applied the 'negative' to the 'scatter' signal so far as his destroyers were concerned, and was upheld in that for he kept his destroyer force intact and ready for any eventuality.

Of course there was an immediate and full-scale inquest at the Admiralty. Mr. Churchill offered as his 'surmise' that the presence of American ships in the escorts and covering force influenced the First Sea Lord into being reluctant to commit them to possible damage. Nothing in the Admiralty investigation, or in the recollection of staff officers concerned, supported this conjecture. The American ships were there to fight and there is no doubt that they would have rendered an adequate account of themselves.

The findings of the inquest have never been fully published, but a shrewd estimate can be made from the First Sea Lord's account given to the Cabinet on 1 August. He said that the Admiralty received information on the night of 3-4 July that *Tirpitz* had eluded our widespread submarine net and 'could be in a position to attack the convoy on the 5th'. Nothing has since come to light to confirm that exact item of information. In fact, the only submarine reports of the German surface units were those made by the Russian submarine which sighted them close into the Norwegian coast around 1700 hours on the 5th, the aircraft sighting them an hour later and finally the submarine *Unshaken* reporting them as turning westwards—that is, for home—at 2030 hours.

The First Sea Lord told the Cabinet that in view of their information the Admiralty (otherwise the First Sea Lord) gave instructions for the convoy to scatter. Mr. Churchill, who was at this Cabinet meeting—he left two or three days later for the Middle East—holds a different view. In Volume IV, page 411, of his History of the Great War, entitled *World Crisis,* he says: 'So strictly was the secret of these orders being sent on First Sea Lord's authority guarded by Admiralty that it was not until after the war that I learned the facts.'

So sparse was the information which came to Admiral Tovey that he did not know until nearly twenty-four hours after the convoy had scattered that the destroyer escort under Commander Broome was supporting Admiral Hamilton and his cruisers. By then, or a few hours earlier, Admiral Tovey had firm intelligence from his submarines that the enemy's heavy ships were close in to North Cape, between 300-350 miles away, having been sighted three or four times. Submarines of the screen were endeavouring desperately to get into position to strike a blow, if not entirely to destroy one or more of the German heavy units, at any rate to slow them down. Unfortunately the attempts failed.

It was too late for C-in-C to do anything about re-forming the convoy. The ships were scattered far and wide over a bleak, merciless sea, and were being hunted down by an equally merciless enemy. Only brief and sometimes incomplete signals gave a clue to their fate.

The inquiry held at the Admiralty brought forth one other peculiar reason for instructing Admiral Hamilton's force to withdraw westward at speed. It was stated that 'information had come to hand that U-boats were concentrating on the cruisers' withdrawal route and it was felt they would constitute a decided danger'. Now U-boats had been hanging on to the skirts of the convoy since the 2nd. That was nothing new. Any PQ convoy in the past eight or nine months had drawn along in its wake a cloud of German submarines. Admiral Hamilton's force, left to its own devices, would not have been unduly alarmed, or seriously threatened. At the speed it could travel, plus the benefit of a destroyer screen, a submarine would be hard placed to get in an attack and would much prefer hunting down a straggler from the convoy.

To summarize the chain of tragic errors related in this chapter does not take long. But somebody blundered, and bundered badly, at the Admiralty. To pass on all intelligence to the forces around PQ17 was quite correct. The movements of the German units most decidedly was a serious threat and the interpretation placed on it was more or less correct. Had it all been passed on to Admiral Tovey, chapter and verse, for him to act upon there could have been no possible vestige of criticism. He might have decided to take the same step, concentrating all his forces available to meet the threat from the German surface units. Or he might even have decided to disperse the convoy into small units, each with its attendant escort. That is conjecture and must remain so.

I put these points recently to a Senior Officer who has known Admiral Tovey all his naval life, and asked if he thought the C-in-C would have ordered the convoy to scatter. The reply was terse. 'Disperse, maybe, if the threat had become really ominous, but disperse to a pattern. Scatter? Not on your bloody life!'

Eight

BUT PQ17 had been scattered.

At the convoy sailing conference a few days previously, the masters of the ships had filed into the conference-room to hear the details of their orders, their positions in the convoy, and to listen to the usual exhortation of a Senior Naval Officer. Part of his ritual was the same for every convoy which ever sailed. 'Do not straggle, gentlemen; keep closed up. If you straggle and lag behind, the convoy has to slow down to wait for you, or an escort has to be detached to cover you, or shepherd you back to the ranks. Remember, a straggler, a lone duck, is a sitting target for U-boat or enemy aircraft.' Finally had come the reassuring words. 'You do your part, gentlemen. Trust the Navy to do its part. It will. Good luck!'

Now the ships were being ordered to scatter, to become lone ducks, sitting targets, a gift for any U-boat or enemy aircraft which came along. And nothing was more certain that they *WOULD* come along. And the Navy? The escorts about which that dogmatic promise had been made? The cruisers and destroyers were steaming away into the flame-tinted west. The other smaller escorts were scattering like leaves blown by an errant puff of wind.

What of the promise? So shocked was Commodore Dowding in SS *River Afton* that on receipt of the signal 'Scatter', he asked for two repeats of it from *Keppel.* Finally, he had to accept the almost unbelievable and pass it on to the ships in his convoy, the convoy which had kept perfect formation throughout three heavy air attacks. Nor indeed had there been any wavering when four ships in its lines had gone up in a sullen rolling cloud of smoke.

Within an hour some of the ships were hull-down on the eastern horizon, some were still clinging together in threes and fours hoping that this temporary cleavage unto one another would offer a crumb of comfort. Within three or four hours the incredulous German pilots, screaming across the sky, blinked, looked again, and began calling up other planes. U-boats, finding no pugnacious escorts steaming between them and the merchant ships, moved in for the kill. And the slaughter began. So, too, did the signals from ships which were being attacked.

'*Empire Byron.* Torpedoed....' '*Earlston.* Attacked by U-boat. ..' '*Pankraft.* Being dive-bombed. Seven bombers. Fighting back....' There were, too, signals which began... but never finished.

Some of the ships had broken away to the east, still within sight of one another, when the Germans struck. Others had broken away towards the south-east, but there was no concealment for them either from the cloudless sky or the brassy sea and the endless daylight.

The 5th of July was but a few hours old when a U-boat sank the *Empire Byron.* A little north of her torpedo-bombers trapped *Earlston,* left her a raddled wreck and swept on to attack the *Washington, Bolton Castle* and *Paulas Potter.* As the torpedo-bombers swept in on the frantically steaming ships a submarine joined in, hit the *Paulus Potter* for a bomber to finish off, as they did the other two. *Pankraft,* which had sheered away from the group of three ships, fared no better. A small group of torpedo-bombers made short work of her, despite the desperate defence from her gunners which sent two bombers tumbling headlong into the sea.

Submarines had moved south and east to cut across the route any ships might take in trying to reach either Matochkin, or Novaya Zemlya, and by midday had discovered, stalked and sunk the Commodore ship *River Afton* and the *Carlton.* At almost the same time another group of sea-wolves had pulled down *Honomu,* torpedoing her. Two hours later they or some other submarines added the *Daniel Morgan* to their swollen bag, while south of that tragedy, bombers had discovered the *Zaafaran, Peter Kerr* and *Fairfield City*—all within a few miles of one another. All these ships had been sunk north of a line drawn from Bear Island to Matochkin Straits. Some of them—the *Washington, Bolton Castle, Earlston* and *Paulus Potter*—were north of the spot where the signal was received to scatter. They were trying to get close to the ice-field in the hope that it would give them some protection, if only from the morning fog which formed as the air rolled over from the ice. The others were just steaming east from the unknown terror astern, the terror which had caused the escorts to turn and leave them and had occasioned the signal to scatter.

Vain hopes in each case.

Steaming south-east, in almost a direct line from Bear Island to Matochkin, steered the anti-aircraft cruiser *Pozarica.* Inevitably, as a lodestone draws metal, so she drew ships towards her and soon had round her a small convoy—a mixed bag of ships. There were the corvettes *Lotus, Poppy, La Malouine* and a couple of merchant ships, one of them *Rathlin* with about sixty-odd survivors from previous sinkings. Captain Lawford, her commanding officer, had only the picture drawn for him by Admiralty signals. Somewhere loose astern of him, it might be right close on his heels, were the German raiders. The convoy had been scattered in order to save itself; forming another convoy was defeating that end. But as *Pozarica* and her little brood steamed fearfully south-east pitiable signals began pouring in from frightened ships seeing imaginary *Hippers.* And one from the Admiralty: 'Most likely time of surface attack now tonight of 5th-6th, or early tomorrow morning, 6 July. Enemy may strike 065 degrees in direction from North Cape.'

At that time the German units had just sailed, and had been reported by a scouting aircraft!

The little company steamed on minus *Lotus,* a little 1,000-ton corvette, armed with one 4-inch gun, commanded by Lieutenant H. J. Hall, RNR. She had turned back to meet whatever fate held in store for her, but bent on rescuing some of the crews of the ships which had been sunk. And fate was kind to the courageous. She found and saved between eighty and ninety men. Eventually she joined up again with *Pozarica.*

Suddenly there was an alarm. Above the razor-sharp

horizon appeared the thin lines of masts. Friend or foe? It was the *Samuel Chase*, an American Liberty ship, which had been attacked and chased by a submarine, but had dodged away in the fog. And she, too, joined the tiny cavalcade. It reached Matochkin Straits to find that it was not the first little impromptu convoy to seek shelter there, for lying in the bleak anchorage was her sister anti-aircraft cruiser *Palomares* who had steered roughly the same course and had acquired a tremulous brood of six ships, among them the fleet minesweepers *Halcyon, Salamander* and *Britomart* and the freighters *Benjamin Harrison* and *El Capitan.*

Other ships, too, had attempted to reach that slender haven of Matochkin, or another nearby inlet in which they could hide from the German surface craft. And they had failed.

On the 6th, German bombers found the *Pan Atlantic* alone. They attacked from three sides, and left her flaming and sinking—her survivors struggling to launch what boats and rafts were not riddled. East of her again, waiting off the Novaya Zemlya coast, were U-boats grimly determined to add to the greatest harvest they had collected throughout the war. And they succeeded.

On the 6 July, when the Admiralty estimated that the convoy would be struck by the German heavy ships (which were by now back secure at anchor), submarines sank the *Hartlebury, Olopana, John Witherspoon* and *Alcoa Ranger.* These four, steaming hard to the south, came against an ice-field off the southern tip of Novaya Zemlya—and were trapped. It was only a small field of ice, much of it mush.

More experienced captains with a knowledge of the Arctic would have slammed through it, and watched the narrow channel close astern of them secure in the knowledge that no U-boat would risk following them. Any Grimsby or Hull semi-explorer semi-fisherman skipper would have done it without thinking twice.

But these freighter captains were not hardy trawlermen inured to the Arctic and its mercilessness. They were accustomed to more temperate waters and were afraid to steam west along the field in case they ran into heavy German units which they still imagined were relentlessly hunting down the remnants of the convoy. The submarines hounded them against the ice-fields like wolves cornering a flock of sheep in a fold. Then they leapt—and slew.

Two ships did round the ice and steam south. They were almost within sight of the Russian coast, a few hours' steaming time from the small port of Iolanka, almost into the entrance to the White Sea, a refuge of sorts where there was established a Russian air-base. For nearly a week they had wriggled southwards only to be caught out by some marauding Heinkels and sunk. It makes sorrowful reading. Of the thirty-six ships which had sailed bravely from Iceland on 29 June twenty-three of them were sunk and two were badly damaged—most of them within twenty-four hours of scattering. Thirteen, including the indomitable *Azerbaidjan*, finally reached Russia, either at Molotovsk or Archangel.

SHIPS SUNK BY 5 JULY

William Hooper, *Christopher Newport*, *Aldersdale* (lost before scattering of convoy), *Washington, Bolton Castle, Paulus Potter, Earlston, Pankraft, Empire Byron, River Afton* (Commodore's ship), *Carlton, Honomu, Zaafaran, Daniel Morgan, Peter Kerr* and *Fairfield City.*

Sunk on the 6 July

Hartlebury

Sunk on the 8 July

John Witherspoon, Olopana and *Alcoa Ranger*

Sunk on the 10 July

Hoosier, El Capitan

The *Azerbaidjan* and the *Winston Salem* were damaged, and the latter went ashore in Novaya Zemlya. They ultimately arrived, but not until twenty-two days after the convoy had ceased to exist as a convoy. Three other ships, *Rathlin, Donbass* and *Bellingham,* steamed through unscathed, helped by a few hours of providential fog which enabled them to put distance between themselves and the holocaust farther north. They arrived at Archangel on 9 July.

There was for a few days ominous silence. *Pozarica* and *Palomares* in Matochkin maintained a rigid radio silence. For them to have been discovered in that anchorage by U-boats and aircraft would have led to a concentrated slaughter. The little band of fugitives had been joined by three of the asdic trawlers, *Lord Austin, Lord Middleton* and *Northern Gem*, and now numbered seventeen ships, six of which were merchant ships. These were *Pozarica, Palomares*; the corvettes *Lotus, Poppy* and *La Malouine;* the fleet minesweepers, *Halcyon, Salamander* and *Britomart*; and the three trawlers. The merchant ships were the *Ocean Freedom, Hoozier, El Capitan, Benjamin Harrison, Samuel Chase* and *Zamalek*—the latter packed with survivors from other ships.

Captain Lawford, commanding *Pozarica*, the Senior Officer, saw the dangers of being trapped and decided to break out and steam close to the island, eventually racing for the entrance to the White Sea. Providentially a fog wrapped itself around the little convoy which sailed on 9 July still shielded by the fog in which *Salamander, Halcyon, Britomart, Ocean Freedom, Samuel Chase* and *Benjamin Harrison* went astray. Only *Ocean Freedom* re-joined. The fog cleared, and the German aircraft came. They were reported on radar sixty miles away . . . fifty miles . . . twenty miles . . . ten miles . . . then they were visible, like savage little hornets buzzing angrily towards the pathetic little cavalcade. For five hours the unofficial convoy fought off a succession of torpedo and bomb attacks. *Zamalek* was straddled time and again, but came rocking through the towering columns of water, still alive, her guns still hitting back. Then *Hoozier* slowed down, swung broadside to the convoy, sinking.

Plane after plane plummeted out of the sky, was pinned in a cone of tracer, was framed in shell-bursts, then hit the sea. But the attack went on as fresh relays of planes arrived. *El Capitan*, an ancient ship of over forty years old, which had sturdily defied the elements in every clime, was hit and began to sink. Only *Ocean Freedom*, of the merchant ships, was left. Desperately the naval ships guarded her, fought off the succession of attacks.

Pozarica broke wireless silence—the Germans knew where the ships were, anyway—and made an anguished appeal for Russian fighters which were only an hour's flight, or less, away. None came. Not one of the Hurricanes the succession of convoys had delivered came out to save the little group of ships some of their travail. And limping along behind finally came *Zamalek*.

At last the German bombers turned away, possibly because they felt they were getting too close to an allied fighter base. Wearily the small convoy re-formed, waiting for *Zamalek* to take up her position, and the deafened, powder-begrimed, wearied-unto-death crews of the naval ships lined their ships' sides and cheered this humble but courageous rescue ship which had done her task come what might. Her skipper, Captain Morris, was awarded the DSO. The missing ships, *Britomart*, *Salamander* and *Halcyon* and their charges, limped in later, having hammered and thrust their way fearfully through the mush-ice south of Novaya Zemlya.

Archangel, bleak even in the brilliant summer sunshine, seemed like heaven to the ships as they slowly secured alongside the quay walls. But the desolating reckoning continued. Only seven or eight ships were accounted for. The remainder? There were suddenly broken signals: 'Am being attacked by dive-bombers. . . .' 'Am being attacked by submarines. . . .' Then nothing more. And there was a possibility that out there in those wide wastes were ships lying disabled, silent, or even survivors of crews making their slow, tortuous way in their lifeboats. Commodore Dowding, himself a survivor from the sunk *River Afton,* decided to begin an investigation. He sailed from Archangel on 16 July in a corvette to search far and wide—but without success. But far to the north of him, three merchant ships were still afloat, still undamaged and still undetected by the Germans, through the ingenuity of the commanding officer of the asdic trawler *Ayrshire.*

She was commanded by Lieutenant Leo Anthony Gradwell, RNVR, in peace-time a barrister, now a respected magistrate at Thames Magistrates' Court, London. His First Lieutenant was a solicitor so *Ayrshire* must have had an entertaining wardroom, particularly as Lieutenant Gradwell had earned the reputation—anyhow in the Navy—of being unorthodox in many respects. In the present tragic circumstances at least, he certainly was. On the order to 'scatter' shortly after 2200 hours on 4 July, *Ayrshire* turned plumb north and steamed hard for the dreaded ice-fields, taking with her three merchant ships, *Silver Sword, Troubadour* and *Ironclad.* On the face of it this was suicidal, for if the German submarines or aircraft spotted them they would have been doomed, trapped as they would have been against the ice. But Gradwell had the answer to that one! I have heard it said, with a degree of authority, that he used to spend some of his peace-time holidays sailing on the large trawlers from Grimsby or Hull into just those waters around Bear Island. He had listened to men of experience and knew, in theory at least, how near he could get to the ice without severely damaging his ship. So with his three precious charges he lined his small convoy closely against the ice. On board, owing to the thrift of his legal colleague, his First Lieutenant, he had a quantity of white and pale green paint, the colours used for disguising—or trying to disguise—escort ships. There was not enough paint for four ships, three of which were large merchant ships, so *Ayrshire's* commanding officer shared it out among them, instructing them to paint only one side—that facing south. Feverishly men slapped the paint on, making the meagre supply go as far as possible. And the job was completed just in time.

Snugly against the ice, concealed by the blink from it and the light paint, the vessels were invisible to the eagerly searching German aircraft which several times ranged far north seeking for remnants from the scattered convoy. At times they were only a few miles from *Ayrshire* and her charges, who watched with bated breath the aircraft flying to and fro. No attacks materialized. When Lieutenant Gradwell, who had been receiving the signals from ships being attacked, estimated that the search and slaughter were taking place farther south, he began nursing his little convoy along the edge of the friendly, concealing ice-field. Finally he turned south until he reached Matochkin on 20 July, utilized the fog around there to slip even farther south, skirted the ice off the tip of Novaya Zemlya and finally—and bravely—steamed his three piebald charges into the White Sea and to safety. Everybody concerned of course had not unnaturally come to the conclusion that *Silver Sword, Troubadour* and *Ironclad* were among those which had been sunk without being able to get off even a part of a signal.

Admiral Tovey's commendation of this piece of work was that it was ingenuity of a very high order. And for it Lieutenant Gradwell was awarded the Distinguished Service Cross.

Eventually the heartbreaking balance-sheet was drawn up. Of the thirty-six merchant ships and two rescue ships which sailed twenty-four had been sunk, two were damaged. Only twelve arrived in Russia—one being *Zamalek*, the rescue ship. It was a disaster of anguishing magnitude, not merely in ships lost, but in prestige—not to mention the degree of triumph which had been handed to the Germans on a silver plate. The loss in material was equally colossal. Eight hundred and ninety-six vehicles were delivered; 3,350 were lost. Of tanks, 164 were delivered; 430 were lost. Eighty-seven aircraft reached Russia; 210 went to the bottom. Of general cargo 57,176 tons were delivered; 100,000 tons were lost.

To bring about this disaster the Germans mounted a full-scale aerial armada: they committed 202 aircraft to the task of destroying PQ17. This force comprised 130 Junkers 88s, forty-three Heinkel 111s and 119s and twenty-nine Heinkel 115s. Of this force a number of machines were damaged, but managed to reach base. Only fifteen were lost. With the exception of a couple of ships sunk and damaged before the convoy scattered, all the damage was done after 2200 hours on 4 July. In addition to the aircraft, eight U-boats were initially committed and after 5 July three more joined in. None was sunk.

What added damning facts to the highly distorted stories circulating around the world was that, in this massacre of PQ17, not one naval ship was lost or seriously damaged. That hideous creature Lord Haw-Haw made much of this feature, and in many a wardroom and mess-deck radio sets were viciously switched off rather than listen to the calumnious twisting of facts.

I remember a puzzled and troubled rating on my ship asking me, after listening to Haw-Haw: 'What really did happen, sir?' I did not know. The fellow's final remark was typical: 'Ah, well, it'll all come out in the wash when the war's over.' What did come out in the 'wash'?

Convoy to Russia. The signal bridge snowed up

HMS *Duke of York* about to fire her 14-inch guns

HMS *Duke of York* in rough water

The ice that had to be chipped from the big guns
just before going into action

A merchant ship bombed on the route for Russia

Rear Admiral R. St Vincent Sherbrooke, VC, CB, DSO.

Captain Jack Broome, DSC, RN.

Heavy seas menace the stern of a British cruiser

Above: Landing on the pitching deck of an aircraft carrier
Centre: An ammunition ship blows up
Below: One Catapult launching and the fighter is 'washed out'

An enemy plane hit by ack-ack

The battleship *Tirpitz*

Nine

EARLY in February 1945 a repatriated American seaman from a German prisoner-of-war camp was lengthily interviewed by an American newspaper and gave a highly coloured account of what happened in the last hours of 4 July 1942. His story carried weight because he was there; he was on a ship which was sunk. And he had been taken from a lifeboat by a U-boat. The interview provoked the Admiralty to issue an official statement giving the full facts [*sic*] of what happened to PQ17. This was the substance of the statement:[1]

'In order to correct erroneous reports recently circulated, the Board of Admiralty have authorized the issue of the following facts concerning the passage of a convoy (PQ17) from the United Kingdom to Russia in July 1942.

'The convoy consisted of 35 supply ships. (*There were in fact thirty-six and two rescue ships.*) Its escort was composed of eleven corvettes, minesweepers and trawlers and two anti-aircraft ships. An additional escort which was provided consisted of six destroyers under command of Commander J. E. Broome in the destroyer *Keppel*.

[1]The italics in parentheses are mine—E. B.

'When the convoy was in a position north-east of Iceland the first cruiser squadron, under command of Admiral L. H. K. Hamilton in HMS *London*, sailed to provide close cover. At about this time aerial reconnaissance revealed that the German battleship *Admiral von Tirpitz* and the cruiser *Admiral Hipper*, in company with a force of destroyers, had sailed from their base in Trondhjem. It was appreciated that this force intended to attack the convoy. In consequence the battle fleet, under command of the Commander-in-Chief, Admiral J. C. Tovey in HMS *Duke of York*, sailed from the United Kingdom.

(Tovey had actually been at sea from the 2nd, following out his regular plan of providing a heavy covering force for the convoy as he had done on previous occasions.)

'Several days passed without event until enemy aircraft were sighted in the vicinity of the convoy and continued to shadow it intermittently. Later a strong force of U-boats were detected in the vicinity.

(Actually a Blohm Voss aircraft picked up the convoy on the evening of 30 *June when close to Jan Mayen Island, not after 'several days'.)*

'One attack was attempted but was beaten off and the voyage was continued with the U-boats remaining in cautious contact. Meanwhile the First Cruiser Squadron steered on a course parallel to the convoy and about forty miles distant from it in the hope that the enemy heavy units might be intercepted.

(This was not an unusual procedure adopted because Tirpitz *and* Hipper *were believed to be out. It was something which was part of C-in-C's usual plan for several of*

the convoys. The cruisers Sheffield, Cumberland, Jamaica, London, Nigeria, Belfast, Trinidad *and* Edinburgh *and one or two others were past-masters in the art of screening a convoy an hour or two's steaming time away, no matter what the weather.*)

'Later there were strong indications that *Admiral von Tirpitz* and *Hipper* were moving in the direction of the North Cape. An attack on the convoy by these heavy ships thus became reasonably certain and the First Cruiser Squadron proceeded to take up disposition accordingly.

(*There is here no mention of the succession of increasingly urgent signals sent to Admiral Hamilton, neither is the excuse—current in* 1942—*that the cruisers were withdrawn because* 'U-boats were concentrating on their return route'.)

'In all the circumstances, it was appreciated that a local tactical situation was developing which was wholly in favour of the enemy.

(*A local situation which seemed to have escaped the attention of C-in-C in* Duke of York *who was still steaming along astern of the convoy and north of Bear Island secure in his intelligence that the German big ships were still* 400 *miles away and close to North Cape. A local tactical situation surely demanded local counter tactics!*)

'Continuous daylight provided him [the enemy] with opportunities for both aerial and surface attack close to occupied territory and with the support of shore-based aircraft and the screen of U-boats.

'That was when the enemy launched his first large-scale attack. Two waves of torpedo-bombers approached the convoy, one from ahead and the other from astern. They were hotly engaged, both by the escorts and by the convoy, and four aircraft were shot down into the sea. The remainder of the enemy force pressed home the attack with great daring and five ships in the convoy were torpedoed and later sank.

(*As a matter of fact three were torpedoed before the order 'Scatter' and one was damaged.*)

'Later, when in a position due north of North Cape, an attack by enemy surface craft seemed imminent, and the convoy was ordered to scatter.

'The six destroyers joined the First Cruiser Squadron to form a balanced striking force.

'An anxious twenty-four hours followed, but no surface attack developed on the scattered ships, this project apparently having been abandoned by the enemy as a result of the dispersion. Meanwhile, the ships of the convoy proceeded independently in small groups towards Russian ports.

(*An anxious twenty-four hours, indeed! Twenty-four hours in which fourteen of the ships were caught out alone, helpless, and sunk.*)

'During this time many of them were subjected to persistent attack by both U-boats and aircraft. During this period nineteen merchant ships were sunk. Nine further enemy aircraft are believed shot down into the sea.

'These attacks were the most severe suffered by any convoy which has made the perilous and fiercely contested passage to and from North Russia.'

This statement was, surprisingly, issued before the war came to an end. Hostilities still had a few months to run. But the mouths of those who were involved—in the Naval ships at least—were still securely sealed. It was a 'wash', a skilful piece of whitewash which skirted facts, avoided dates and clouded main issues very brilliantly.

It was five years later that one of the men involved, and one able to reveal such pertinent facts (Captain Broome, erstwhile Commander Broome of *Keppel*), broke into brief print, and justifiably so.

The BBC, on 2 October 1949, broadcast a feature programme called *The Battle of the Atlantic*, written and narrated by Chester Wilmot and produced by Laurance Gilliam. And Captain Broome took exception to some of the facts related in the programme about PQ17.

'It seems [he wrote] now and then this tragedy is trotted out, laughed off, and then locked up in its cupboard. On this occasion the BBC was the medium. The fact that it was a disaster was excused by the expression: "being wise after the event". Although some of the facts were as given quite true, *the biggest fact of all was left out.*

'It was I (as Senior Officer Escort) in command of the close escort in HMS *Keppel* who received that signal "to scatter the convoy forthwith".

'Nelson's famous signal as he led his team into battle at Trafalgar has become a legend. The signal ordering me to scatter that convoy should also be a legend—below the line.

'IT WAS MADE FROM A DESK 2,000 MILES FROM MY BRIDGE. It is carved in every book of fighting rules that desks *advise* bridges—they pass them information, they report situations, they route, they help in every way they can

. . . *but they do not give orders.* Tactical orders can only be given by the man on the bridge.

'Scattering a convoy is the last tactical step taken by the man on the spot to disperse and complicate the convoy target in the *presence of the enemy.* (*As with* Jervis Bay—E. B.)

'*No enemy was present.*

'Just imagine what it felt like on my bridge, having scattered the convoy, when no enemy appeared, when it was too late to round the convoy up again. It was lack of wisdom *during the event* that caused the disaster.'

A hundred thousand words could be written about the PQ17 disaster, and yet could say nothing more eloquently than what Captain Broome has said. Somebody at a desk 2,000 miles away blundered. He was not finished. A passage in Sir Winston Churchill's *World Crisis* spurred him into more print on the same theme.

Sir Winston, whose recollections do, at times, seem slightly cloudy said, in writing of PQ17: 'Unfortunately the destroyers of the convoy escort also withdrew (with the cruisers)'.

Captain Broome wrote to the Editor, *Daily Telegraph*, on 30 October 1950 thus:

'This statement may reasonably create the impression that the destroyer force was free to remain with the convoy or withdraw.

'It was from no misfortune that the destroyers under my command withdrew. *It resulted from a direct order from the Admiralty to scatter the convoy.* This order could only have been justified by the proximity of the enemy, and it demanded therefore that I should concentrate my destroyer force with the nearby cruisers.

'The responsibility for the tragic events which followed must rest with those who, in contradiction to naval practice, elected to direct an Arctic convoy from London, instead of passing information and leaving the decisions to the commander on the spot.'

Can more be written on this tragic theme of PQ17? No. Of the courage of British naval ships escorting subsequent convoys to Russia? Quite a lot.

Ten

THE inquests, the recriminations and the percussions following the massacre of PQ17 began to die away. . . . But one fact remained. Russia, now forcing Germany to enter a second winter of war, was stridently urging that more and more supplies be sent. A perhaps over-simplified way of looking at their attitude was this: A convoy which started out was destroyed; very well, send another one! And should that one be cut to pieces, then send yet another! Russia was throwing whole armies into the path of the Germans and was ruthlessly sacrificing them to slow down, to clog, the wheels of the Wehrmacht.

The frozen-eyed, ex-Georgian killer, Stalin, measured not effort in terms of effort, neither did he know the meaning of the word sacrifice. He was interested only in final results. How many stores, tanks, bombers and ammunition are being sent? How much arrives? And what arrived, in his eyes, was not enough. The value of helping the Russians was not unrecognized in this country and America. It was not, once again to reiterate, pure altruism. The greater the Russian effort, the greater would be the amount of attrition until we, America and Great Britain, were ready to hit the Germans in the West. But there had to be a limit somewhere to the wastage of ships, both naval and merchant.

Anglo-American political pressure from the comparative security of an office desk was being applied to the Admiralty to run another convoy in late August or early September to replace all the material lost in PQ17. Churchill urged the C-in-C Home Fleet to put forth a further and intensive effort to solve the problem of running convoys by this deadly northern route. In typical Churchillian phrases it was suggested that a convoy be sent on a more southerly route instead of skirting the ice-pack and keeping north. The convoy would steam bravely close to the tip of the Norwegian coast and would be 'fought through' with an air umbrella provided by all available fleet and escort carriers, plus an extremely strong surface escort both close to the convoy and in the wings waiting for a cue to enter.

In theory, splendid! In fact, the Admiralty, and particularly Admiral Tovey, had only one word for it—MURDER!

It would mean, at the least, five or six days of endless fighting against goodness only knows what German surface craft, innumerable U-boats and successive relays of German bombers and torpedo-planes. The Germans could be relied upon to produce a maximum effort both on, above and under the sea for such a prize. The triumph over PQ17 was obviously still fresh in their minds, and over a period the Germans had considerably augmented their naval forces in north Norway. The battleship *Tirpitz* and destroyers were at Trondhjem; the *Lützow*, another pocket-battleship, the cruisers *Admiral Hipper*, *Köln*, *Nürnberg* and destroyers were either at Narvik or Altenfiord; and the battle-cruiser *Scharnhorst* and the cruiser *Prinz Eugen* and a flotilla of destroyers were expected to move up from the Baltic at any time. If only a part of this fleet was sailed against a convoy, courageously steaming across the Germans' own doorstep, the result would be a foregone conclusion. PQ17 would look like a brief Saturday afternoon excursion compared with it. But political expediency demanded another convoy be sailed and planning went on.

Arranging a convoy, even on the most favourable route (if such a thing could exist at all in a war), meant a tremendous effort, but the planning for PQ18 transcended anything that had been done previously. While the cargoes were being routed to the various docks around Great Britain, and the ships—some of them still at sea in other convoys—were being earmarked, the Admiralty, strenuously backed up by Admiral Tovey, resisted the idea of a straight dash across the tip of Norway. Apart from PQ17, which as we have seen had been the victim of a tragic error, they had had experience of convoys being 'fought through' at Malta. On some of those convoys losses amounted to more than eighty per cent of the merchant ships, and fifty per cent of the escorts sunk or damaged. Finally, the idea of the straight dash was abandoned on condition that a convoy was arranged.

Before that could be formed and sailed, we had a force of ships, minesweepers and escort ships and aircraft languishing in Russian ports bereft of stores and ammunition which had been lost in PQ17. There had to be stores replacements for them. Four destroyers were sailed with urgent, vital stores in July. And got through safely. This did not imply that the Germans were relaxing on that northern route; on the contrary, they had a dozen or more patrolling submarines watching off Bear Island besides unceasing air patrols. But four destroyers, steaming at twenty-five knots plus, was a smaller far more elusive target than a slow, unwieldy convoy of merchant ships.

The big problem which presented itself well in the forefront was some increase in air cover and a larger striking power in the air at the Barents Sea end of the run. The Russians had promised fighter aircraft—but it was a promise yet to be fulfilled.

The German naval forces in north Norway could be attacked by heavy bombers if, and only if, the machines could fly on to a base in Russia to refuel for another strike. To strengthen this striking-force a number of torpedo-bombers would have to be based in north Russia with stores, equipment and ground staff. The Russians, enigmatic and puzzling, agreed to this very reluctantly. They could not, or would not, see that this arrangement for an air striking-force was as essential as the convoys themselves. They seemed to think that if planes could be flown or carried to Russia, then they should be handed over to them for their undeniably great struggle.

Admiral Tovey decided to ferry these essential stores in a purely naval convoy. The US cruiser *Tuscaloosa* and three British destroyers were sailed from the Clyde on 13 August with men and equipment for Nos. 144 and 455 Squadrons of Hampdens. The convoy got through.

Now comes the completely inexplicable attitude taken up by the Russians. If they make one concession they refuse to make another, regardless of the merits of the case. On the

Tuscaloosa was a well-equipped British medical unit which sailed to look after the sick and wounded who had survived PQ17 and other convoys, and for whom there were absolutely no facilities at all. The Russians neither provided any nor would allow any. They refused to permit the medical unit to land. It was not just a question of an original 'no' with an ultimate grudging 'yes'. It was '*niet*', flat and final. The mission therefore had to return, while British and American seamen were critically ill, lacking every form of medical and surgical attention except what could be provided by the extremely limited facilities of the ships in Archangel. Some day—but one doubts it—the Russians may offer an explanation.

Early in September, thirty-two Hampden torpedo-bombers took off from this country for Russia. Six crashed in Norway or Sweden; two lost their way and were badly damaged making fuelless landings in Russia. And one, reaching Kola Inlet, saw thankfully Russian fighters closing in on it. Safety at last! Then the fighters promptly shot it down! Following the Hampdens went four Spitfires and finally, No. 210 Squadron of Catalinas, invaluable long-range seaplanes. So by early in September there was in north Russia a balanced force of striking and reconnaissance aircraft under the command of Group Captain F. L. Hopps, RAF.

While all this preparation was going on, planning was in progress for the main reason for it—a convoy! The idea was to sail convoy PQ18 outwards and QP14 homewards with such survivors of previous convoys as were fit to sail.

German radio intelligence had estimated that we were

about to run the gauntlet yet once more—sailing, in fact, two convoys. They also estimated roughly where we planned to have the convoys pass one another—not a very difficult task. We would have to arrange a maximum naval effort and covering force for that vital stretch of water between Bear Island and the tip of Norway. It would be immediately prior to that that the Germans would begin their attacks, and would continue them through and into the Barents Sea. U-boats and destroyers were sent out in a sortie, and the minelayer *Ulm* was despatched to lay mines at the eastern end of the run, at the entrance to the White Sea. They all had orders that if they sighted either convoy they were to hang on to it, report it and wait for larger forces to attack. *Ulm*, incidentally, paid for her temerity. She was caught out south-east of Bear Island by the destroyers screening the returning *Tuscaloosa* and was expeditiously sunk in a very short time.

Admiral Tovey came to the conclusion that covering convoy PQ18 with heavy ships after it had passed Bear Island did not provide an effective screen. The heavy ships, deep into enemy territory, would have to have with them a substantial destroyer screen, particularly if some emergency compelled them to sail farther east than planned. He decided that the destroyers could be used to better advantage as an outlying escort, strengthening the close escort around the convoy. It was recognized that it was almost inevitable that the convoy would be sighted and reported, and that it would be subjected to a long and stern fight.

A formidable escort and covering force were assembled as the convoy was slowly being formed in Loch Ewe. It was placed under the command of Rear-Admiral R. L. (Bob) Burnett, Admiral (D) flying his flag in the cruiser *Scylla.* Under his command he had sixteen fleet destroyers which were to cover PQ18 and QP14 through the valley of death east and west of Bear Island, and into the western portion of the Barents Sea. The close escort, which would stick by the convoy, come-what-may, comprised two destroyers, two anti-aircraft ships, four corvettes, three fleet minesweepers, four asdic trawlers and three submarines. Also attached was *Avenger,* an escort carrier and two destroyers. In short, this was the largest escort yet assembled for a Russian convoy.

Let us array the ships in detail.

There was the close escort of eighteeen ships; the escort carrier *Avenger* and two destroyers; then came the fighting destroyer escort, *Scylla* and her sixteen destroyers; the cruiser covering force *Norfolk,* flying the flag of Admiral Bonham-Carter, *Suffolk, London, Cumberland* and *Sheffield* and another destroyer. Finally, the distant covering force of *Anson,* flying Vice-Admiral Sir John Fraser's flag, *Duke of York* and the cruiser *Jamaica* with five destroyers. Fifty-one warships flying the White Ensign at sea to try to ensure that PQ18 would be fought through.

Of course, many of those ships would not become embroiled unless the Germans entered the arena with a strong surface unit of heavy ships. Attacks by U-boats and aircraft would have to be the task of the close escort, the escort carrier and *Scylla's* destroyers, if necessary. All this effort, all this planning, went to ensure not only that a convoy of thirty-nine ships now forming in Loch Ewe would have a fighting chance of completing the trip, but that another convoy, QP14, could return.

Although it is scarcely the right expression to use, the bait (that is, PQ18) was there and so far as the naval forces were concerned it has naturally always been a source of much regret that the Germans did not commit a heavy force to the attack when it came. Had they sailed *Lützow*, *Hipper* and *Scheer* with a cloud of destroyers there would have been a naval battle of gargantuan proportions. But we are getting ahead of our story. . . .

The usual plan of arranging for outward- and homeward-bound convoys to pass near Bear Island was varied. QP14 was timed to leave when PQ18 was nearing the end of its run. This threw a greater strain on the covering ships, but it was an accepted risk. The convoy was originally routed to sail north of Bear Island but ice-fields changed that. So on 2 September the convoy sailed. Slowly the ships steamed out of Loch Ewe, formed up, and steered north through the Minches into the open sea, and the Commodore formed them into the compact column formation they would endeavour to maintain to the end of the voyage, weather and enemy permitting. Six days later, east of Iceland, the escorts and screening forces formed up around them either in close escort or not far away.

Discovery by the Germans was almost inevitable; they knew of the convoy's estimated route—it would have to be from Iceland—and steer as it might it would ultimately have to close to the tip of Norway. The Germans disposed three groups of submarines (about eighteen in all) across the estimated route, and one of the groups was not long in reporting the convoy. It was located, in fact, on the day the escort and screening force took up positions. But there was no attack.

Once the Germans knew that the convoy had sailed, they had to do their own planning. In addition to the submarines hanging on to the skirts of the convoy, the inevitable lone aircraft appeared and circled but kept out of range of the guns of the escort. The 10th of September dawned—a mere figure of speech, this, because darkness only lasted three hours or so—and the Admiralty Intelligence reported movements of German heavy craft from Altenfiord. *Scheer, Hipper* and *Köln* and their attendant destroyers had sailed. The British submarine *Tigris,* on patrol off Norway, got in one attack but unfortunately missed and was severely and lengthily counter-attacked, forcing her to remain submerged so that she could not report the course and speed of the enemy.

The Germans planned first to steer east, seek out QP14, which by normal planning should by then be nearing Bear Island. It would then hammer the convoy which would, they hoped, have the effect of drawing whatever heavy ships we had well to the east, dodge them, and then retrace their course west and hit PQ18. Hitler for some reason felt that this would be risking his heavy ships too much, and so placed a veto on the plan. In any event they would have been combing empty seas because QP14 had not sailed. But the fact that the German heavy ships were at sea was menacing. Was it a short feint, such as the one which led to the débâcle around PQ17, or was this a genuine punitive sortie? The British forces and convoy plugged north-east—tense, waiting, escorts slipping in to supply-tankers to fuel-up, watching warily for any optimistic U-boat which might feel inclined to take a hand.

The 11th of September came with the strain becoming almost unbearable. Reports of U-boats and the persistent aircraft told them that they had been reported, and they realized that there would be an attack. But what were the Germans waiting for? The heavy craft to get into position? Was it to be a three-part attack? U-boats, aircraft and pocket-battleships and cruisers? Still there was no attack.

In the light of subsequent events it is obvious that there was a lack of co-operation between the German navy and the Luftwaffe. Each knew of the presence of the convoy, but each decided to mount its own attack. By this time there were more than twenty U-boats strung out along the route—a formidable force. The Germans had available niney-two torpedo-bombers and 133 long-range or dive-bombers; and were prepared to commit practically all of them. The Luftwaffe knew that there was an aircraft-carrier with the convoy, and planned that when they did start attacking they would concentrate on her first.

The 12th came—with first blood to the British escorts. Aboard the destroyer *Faulkner* the asdic operator, with his headphones clamped to his ears, suddenly let out a yelp. 'Contact! ' The submarine attack team went smoothly into operation. The contact was firmly held; *Faulkner*, ahead of the convoy, swung into action. The torpedo-gunner and his depth-charge crews aft patted the grey, sinister canisters before they went over the side. Suddenly the sea astern of her erupted into towering columns of water, a glistening, porpoise-shaped hull rolled sluggishly amid the maelstrom. Another attack—and there was one submarine less to harass the convoy.

Now the weather began to take a hand. Banks of fog rolled over the convoy, occasional squalls of blinding snow ripped through it. And the masters of the ships in the convoy and the escorts permitted themselves a bleak smile. This was weather that they had once detested, but nowadays welcomed. To keep in touch with the mass of shipping, the U-boats would have to close in, and there were other destroyers eager and anxious to repeat *Faulkner's* feat. Frustrated aircraft could be heard droning overhead, powerless to tell whether or no the convoy had seized the opportunity to change course.

On the 13th—ominous date! —the weather cleared and by the forenoon the Germans had made contact again. And this was no shadowing move; the U-boat packs closed in. . . . A ship in the starboard column suddenly staggered. A gout of smoke and flame belched up from her side. Then another reeled away. The U-boats had struck. Around both sides of the convoy depth-charges split the waters and hammered at the wolf-pack. The escorts and the merchant ships had no illusions: the first attack had been beaten off, but most of their crews were veterans of the Battle of the Atlantic and the Gibraltar run. They knew that these submarines would attack again and again from every angle—from ahead, from each side and from astern.

An hour or two later another attack began, this time a combined submarine and aircraft effort, although the aircraft involved were not in any great strength. The escorts slammed the submarines, each racing outwards to every contact, depth-charging it mercilessly, then turning to race back again to its position in the screen. There was no means of knowing how many of the attacks on the U-boats were successful. The primary object was of course to drive them down deep so that if they survived they would be forced to manœuvre again for another position.

Against the few German aircraft *Avenger* launched some of her Sea Hurricanes, blood-sisters to the aircraft which had written history in the sky in the summer of 1940. The Hurricanes swept across the head of the convoy—lean, swift, sinister, lethal. And the German air attack faded for the time being, and there were no further losses in the convoy.

The next air attack was made by JU88s. An intense barrage was put up by the escorting ships and the merchantmen. Only one ship was hit and the JUs turned away. Tracer filled the sky, the burst of anti-aircraft shells pitted it with grey-black blobs until it seemed impossible that aircraft could fly through it and live. But they did. *Avenger's* Hurricanes twisted and turned, sometimes fighting half a dozen enemy planes at the same time. Thin streamers of black smoke began from a pinpoint in the sky then broadened as a plane—a speck of red at the beginning of the smoke—hit the water. There was no time to see whether it was enemy or friend.

U-boats wriggled frenziedly through the ranks of the escorts, fired a fan of torpedoes and then twisted away. And counter-attack after counter-attack were made by the escort ships. . . . The JU88s again turned away, but only to allow room for the torpedo-bombers to skim over the water to launch their deadly weapons. These machines, forty of them, came in low on the starboard side, flying through an intense barrage. Having fired their weapons, they then swung away. The attack lasted less than ten minutes, but only one ship from the starboard column survived. Eight were left sinking, some on fire. 'Fighting the convoy through' had become more than a mere figure of speech.

Eleven

THE few meagre hours of darkness—if a deep greyness of the sky can be so called—brought little relief to the escorts which had to turn away frequently to counter-attack against daring submarines. One ship fell to the U-boats shortly after midnight on the 14th—the oiler *Athel Templar.* In the half-darkness *Avenger* launched some Swordfish planes and between them and the destroyer *Onslow* the probable slayer of the oiler was sunk. It was U-589.

The north-east sky was tinted with a lighter grey, then it became flame tinged as the sun prepared to take over for the next twenty hours. Tired and unshaven, every bone in their bodies aching from exhaustion, and their heads still ringing with the previous day's bombardment, the men of the merchant and naval ships roused themselves to meet the new day. At about this time came a wave of acute anxiety at the Admiralty, and at Scapa. The RAF reported that its planes had failed to locate *Tirpitz* at Narvik—or anywhere else. Had she sailed to join in the onslaught, the massacre of yet another convoy? Roughly the same situation was building up around PQ18 as that which led to the naval forces being withdrawn from PQ17.

Pulses quickened in the heavy surface units at sea, astern

and south of the convoy. The cruiser screening force flexed its muscles and Admiral Burnett's sixteen destroyers licked their jowls in anticipation of something larger than a submarine to attack. Nevertheless, the position was acute. *Tirpitz*, and possibly another heavy craft and a flotilla of destroyers, could appear from anywhere and do immeasurable damage to the convoy before being brought to fight with our heavy forces. *Scylla*, of course, although a cruiser, was armed with 4.7 guns, and for that reason was rather irreverently known at Scapa Fow as The Toothless Terror, because of her stumpy 4.7 guns fitted to her 6-inch turrets.

Tirpitz and a surface force did not appear, although any distant cloud of smoke was viewed with some apprehension for a day or two. The threat was always there. In actual fact, *Tirpitz* eventually returned to her anchorage on the 18th after exercising in the safe waters of Vestfiord.

During the morning hours the convoy was attacked by submarines, but they were desultory assaults and no ships were sunk or damaged. The German pilots of course had roughly about 400 miles to fly back to their base for re-fuelling. They had given up the attack the previous evening, possibly returned home to a few toasts to their mutual successes and a night's sleep while their planes were being repaired, re-fuelled and rearmed. Shortly after midday they began a fresh attack, and in the initial stages concentrated both on the aircraft-carrier *Avenger*, whose Sea Hurricanes were such a thorn in the side of the Luftwaffe, and anti-aircraft ship *Ulster Queen*.

Wisely, their commanding officers felt that so long as their ships were close to the convoy their manœuvres were restricted, so they moved away to take advantage of the room in which to use their extra speed. *Avenger* tore obliquely across the van of the convoy, peeling off Hurricanes in a vicious little swarm against the JU88s and torpedo-bombers. The Germans had launched this attack in three layers—torpedo-bombers first, then JU88s above them, followed by another layer, low down, of torpedo-carrying aircraft. Between the escorts and the Sea Hurricanes, twenty-two German aircraft were shot down—thirteen torpedo-bombers and nine JU88s. One merchant ship was hit and disabled. She was obviously sinking so she was finished off by a destroyer. A sad, but necessary, task.

Again there were a few relatively peaceful hours during the half-darkness, although the escort and screening forces were on the alert in case of an attack by *Tirpitz* and her accompanying ships at first real light. U-boats tried an attack or two but without success, and the destroyer *Impulsive* sank one which had the temerity to get in too close. A couple of waves of bombers—about fifty in all—attacked but wilted away from the intense anti-aircraft fire from all the ships, as well as from *Avenger's* bloodthirsty Sea Hurricanes which considered it a poor fight if they were not individually taking on four or five bombers apiece at the same time. And there were no casualties among the ships in the convoy, except from near-misses and splinters. No ships were sunk or disabled badly enough to compel them to fall out of station. For the rest of the day there was neither attack nor threat of one, except from the dozen or so submarines hanging on like wolves fringing a herd of cattle.

In the afternoon of the 15th Admiral Burnett and part of his destroyer force left PQ18 to assume a protective role over QP14 which had now sailed and which was on its way towards Bear Island. To offset this to some extent four Russian destroyers joined the escort force for PQ18, whilst Catalinas from north Russia flew submarine-discouraging-patrols around the convoy.

It looked as if PQ18 was going to be sailed in without further loss; but then on the 18th, when the convoy was almost into the White Sea, the Germans attacked again with clouds of torpedo-bombers and JU88s, fuelling up and reloading no doubt at Petsamo. This was a vicious, sustained attack pushed home against fierce anti-aircraft fire put up by the indignant gunners of all the ships. One more ship reeled away in flames to sink—almost in sight of its destination. Four enemy aircraft were shot down. A brief attack was also launched as the ships were breaking up convoy formation on the morning of the 24th—it was blowing half a gale or more and visibility was very poor. The attack was not thrust home and no ships were hit or sunk. Of the forty ships which sailed from Loch Ewe on 2 September twenty-seven of them arrived, which meant a grievous loss of thirteen ships. Had that number been lost through bad weather in one whole winter in the Atlantic in peace-time it would have shocked the world. But by the time PQ18 sailed we had become inured to such severe losses which made no great emotional stress on the planners, who didn't have to sail in them or escort them, anyway. We were accustomed to convoys losing ten, twelve, or fifteen ships.

PQ18 had been fought through, but at a tremendous cost.

It is doubtful if any convoy ever had such a powerful escort and screening force, and to sail repeated convoys at frequent intervals would inevitably exhaust escort crews completely; moreover, many of the ships used were urgently needed elsewhere for other commitments. Admiral Tovey argued and argued against obdurate opinions held elsewhere that a forty-ship convoy, or even a thirty-ship, was too big, too unwieldy. If it suffered bad weather it was scattered over a couple of hundred square miles, and the task of rounding it up took more time from the hard-worked escorts. Furthermore, it allowed the U-boats and aircraft wider scope in attacking individual ships, as in the case of PQ17.

The Admiral's ideal size was around fifteen to eighteen ships—a compact, small convoy which could be handled by the escort, manœuvred more easily and therefore could stand a better chance of getting through with small losses. The escort need not be so large, yet it would be quite as effective. How right he was we shall see later!

One stern lesson was learned from the attacks on PQ18. Sailing convoys to Russia in the summer hours of endless daylight was a project highly spiced with danger. Had the German heavy surface craft sailed on a punitive foray they would have had all day—guided by aircraft—in which to locate their prey, position themselves for a devastating attack which would annihilate the merchant ships and many of the light escorting craft, and possibly avoid any fight at all with our heavy ships. This was a possibility to be considered for the three days that *Tirpitz* was 'lost'. Even if they were brought to fight against our battleships and cruisers, the primary reason for it all (the convoys) might have been destroyed. As it was, the fight over PQ18 was largely one of repeated aircraft attack to the well-known formula of bombers first, followed by torpedo-bombers with bombers coming in again.

The submarines, of course, stage-managed their own attacks apparently independent of the aircraft. They sank three ships, and aircraft sank ten, for a loss of forty bombers and three submarines. The lesson was there for all to see. Even with half a hundred fighting ships either close-herding the convoy or screening it in the vicinity, there was always the possibility, during the long summer days and nights, of a convoy being cut to ribbons.

Tirpitz and *Hipper*, with a flotilla of destroyers, could be homed on a convoy by submarines or aircraft, and could shell it to smithereens. The escorting destroyers and the outer screen of cruisers would have to be sacrificed in an attempt to save some of the convoy. It was too much to hope for that a couple of cruisers and a few destroyers could beat off such a heavy raid if it were thrust home with any determination. It was something considered beyond the realms of possibility. Yet that is precisely what happened.

If the partly told story of the débâcle of PQ17 left a bitter taste—and the rumours and garbled versions circulating around the world increased the bitterness—then the story of convoy JW51B must have done something to lessen that bitterness. . . .

So on to the battle around JW51B, an epic measured by any standard.

Twelve

THE holocaust of PQ17 and the slaughter of PQ18 were bitter memories. It is doubtful if Stalin's naval experts were yet convinced that sailing convoys over that northern route in the long summer and early autumn nights was inviting a continuation of the tragic losses. Admiral Tovey and the rest of the Navy certainly knew it.

At all events it was decided to wait until there were longer hours of darkness, and the savage winter weather, bad as it was, would offer some protection. No outward convoys were sailed until December, then two were arranged. Thirty ships were gathered together at Loch Ewe, and after some acidulated exchanges of correspondence it was decided to sail the convoy in two parts. The designations were altered from PQ and QP for the outward and homeward convoys to JW51 for the outward- and RA for the homeward-bound.

The first convoy to attempt the run with the protection of bad weather was actually QP15 which sailed from the White Sea on 17 November. Admiral Tovey, who by now must have become very tired indeed of trying to convince higher authority that he and his experienced captains knew what they were talking about, and knew what was best, wanted it to be limited to a maximum of twenty ships. As in the past he was overruled and the convoy sailed twenty-eight ships strong. They were in ballast, carrying no cargo—and what Admiral Tovey had feared, happened. The ships ran into a series of heavy gales, were unable to keep station and just ceased being a convoy. They were scattered over hundreds of square miles, and the escorting destroyers sent to meet them found the job almost impossible. The merchant ships, battling against tremendous seas and demoniacal winds, with their propellers out of the water half the time, struggled along towards Iceland independently.

The only fragment of comfort that Admiral Tovey could have derived from the punishing conditions was that the same weather which had smashed the convoy also hampered the German U-boats and enemy aircraft reconnaissance. U-boats did, however, locate two ships, more by luck than judgment, and sank them. Some of the ships struggled along at less than two knots, in forty-eight hours 'over the ground' making less than one hundred miles. One Liberty ship broke in two parts and the hard-pressed, overworked destroyers, trying to find the scattered remnants of the convoy, set to work in the foulest weather imaginable, to get tows to the two halves and towed them into harbour. This was an epic performance. Destroyers at slow speeds in bad weather are not the easiest of ships to handle. They have the relative length and breadth of a lead pencil, and can whip through a near-ninety degrees roll with a breathtaking plunging pitch added in a matter of a few seconds.

But QP15 finally arrived in port in its several parts and with, on the final reckoning, only two ships lost. This was at least something of a vindication for Admiral Tovey's oft-repeated dictum that bad weather could be used as an ally. Whether the obdurate higher authority finally accepted this or not, or whether further planning occupied their time, is not recorded.

The next convoys to sail outward-bound were the two parts of JW51, although Admiral Tovey had wanted to emphasize his point by sailing a small convoy of six heavily escorted ships, late in November or early December. His hope and intention were to sail a succession of small convoys (each a maximum of ten ships) so that he could provide escorts of four destroyers and arrange for other screening craft. In the light of experience there is little doubt that this would have been the most profitable course. Although there was never a superabundance of destroyers and light cruisers available to the Home Fleet, Admiral Tovey was now relatively well off compared with his recent poverty. The ships that he had contributed to the invasion of Africa were now returning to him, some battle-scarred, all veterans with strange nostalgic thoughts of Gibraltar, North Africa and other places where the sun shines even in winter.

The original suggestion was that JW51 should sail as one convoy or as smaller units sailing so closely together that in effect they would be one long-drawn-out convoy. Admiral Tovey disagreed strenuously. The fact that QP15, weather-beaten and scattered, had emerged comparatively unscathed with a loss of only two ships was sheer luck. . . .

There were discussions as well as a visit by his Chief of Staff to London, and eventually Admiral Tovey was ordered to sail the convoy in two parts—sixteen ships apiece, escorted by seven destroyers and smaller craft with two 6-inch cruisers to cover them in the Barents Sea. The cruisers allocated for this task were the 9,000-ton *Sheffield*, commanded by Captain A. W. Clarke, and the *Jamaica*. The first part of the convoy, designated JW51A, duly sailed on 15 December and arrived at Murmansk on Christmas Day. It had not been attacked and all ships were undamaged, even by weather. The Germans registered their disapproval of this success by staging an ineffective air raid from one of their air bases at Petsamo or Kirkenes, which were only ninety miles away. As a result of the well-earned Christmas celebrations, perhaps the anti-aircraft fire provided by the ships and their escorting destroyers, plus the cruisers *Sheffield* and *Jamaica*, might have been a trifle erratic; but at least they made what the psalmist calls 'a joyful noise' and some thoroughly chastened German airmen returned to their belated Christmas lunch in thoughtful mood. On Boxing Day the two cruisers and their destroyers, *Opportune* and *Matchless*, sailed to get into their screening position for convoy JW51B which was then approaching Jan Mayen Island.

JW51B had been assembled at Loch Ewe, that bleak marshalling area for nearly all convoys. It sailed on 22 December, fourteen ships in all—four of them British, nine American and one flying the blue-and-red ensign of Panama, under convoy Commodore Captain R. A. Melhuish, late of the Indian Navy. After the convoy conference, which was attended by Captain Robert St. Vincent Sherbrooke,[1] Captain (D.) of the 17th Destroyer Flotilla, the destroyers sailed

[1]Actually, his name is 'Rupert', but throughout the Navy and in his family circle he is known as, and prefers, Robert,—E.B.

independently for Seidisford, Iceland, and the escort which was to conduct it there began the job of marshalling the convoy which was later destined to make naval history—or at least take part in it.

Here I must interject a personal note: the senior ship of the close escort was the minesweeper *Bramble,* Commander H. T. Rust, DSO, in command. The full escort was *Bramble,* three Hunt-class destroyers, *Blankney, Chiddingfold* and *Ledbury,* two corvettes, *Hyderabad* and *Rhododendron,* and an Algerine-class fleet sweeper *Circe,* with two trawlers as Tail-end Charlies and rescue ships, *Northern Gem* and *Vizalma.*

A couple of weeks previously I had commissioned a new minesweeping asdic ship, a neat, compact little craft and, by an odd coincidence, both *Circe* and *Bramble* were, as they say in Ireland, adjacent. The First Lieutenant of *Circe* and her Gunnery Officer were Lieutenant 'Nicky' Near, RNR, and Lieutenant Noel Neely, RNVR, old comrades of mine from early days at Dover. Two officers of *Bramble* were also old friends. We foregathered. That day, after having languished long under a combination of dark grey and red anti-corrosive paint, some painters descended on my new ship and gave her a face lift. She was painted white and pale green in a wondrous design. The *Bramble-Circe* confederacy gloomily forecast that such exotic colouring made us practically a certainty for Iceland, and a firm favourite for Murmansk. As veterans of those waters they regaled my young wardroom personnel (and the open-eared stewards) with fearsome tales. We parted—to meet again briefly at Loch Ewe; they bound north, we bound south with a portion of a convoy for the Bristol Channel. As we sailed, *Bramble* sent us a signal: 'We'll give your love to Katinka.' Nine days later Bramble was to sail off into the murk, and her fate was to remain a mystery until the end of the war, when it was learned that she had gone down in action against a German cruiser and a destroyer.

JW51B sailed from Loch Ewe for Iceland in threatening weather. Leading was *Empire Archer*, the Commodore ship, loaded with 4,500 tons of war material, 140-odd lorries, eighteen tanks and twenty-one crated fighter aircraft. Next was *Daldorch*, with nearly 1,800 tons of mixed cargo, all war equipment, 260-odd lorries and other sundries. Third was *Empire Emerald*, a lethal ship if ever there was one. Her crew lived over 7,400 tons of high-octane aviation spirit and 2,500 tons of fuel oil. One little flaming tracer-bullet, a couple of inches long, ripping through her thin hull could turn her into a gigantic blazing brand in seconds. The fourth, also a tanker, was loaded with the same dangerous cargo. She was the *Pontfield*. A fifth British ship, the *Dover Hill*, developed an engine defect and did not sail with the convoy.

Then came the American contingent. First was the *Executive*. Stowed below she had 130 lorries, 4,000 tons of war cargo and lashed on deck, in crates, were four bombers. Astern of her was the *Puerto Rican*, with 5,000 tons of cargo comprising tanks, fighters, bombers and lorries—either stowed below or lashed on her upper decks. The *Vermont* was similarly loaded. Behind *Vermont* came the Rear-Commodore ship, the *Jefferson Myers*, with 370 lorries and 6,000 tons of cargo stowed in her holds and four big bombers, crated, on her foredeck. Following came the Vice-

Commodore ship, second-in-command in control of the convoy, the *Calobre*, then the *John H. B. Latrobe*, the *Ballot* (flying the Panama flag, but chartered to the United States Maritime Commission), the *Chester Valley*, the *Yorkmar* and the *Ralph Waldo Emerson.*

Captain Sherbrooke and his destroyers had sailed ahead of the convoy to fuel up at Seidisford for the long trip through the Barents Sea. They would next see the convoy at a rendezvous about 150 miles east of Iceland. Once clear of the Butt of Lewis, the bad weather promised by the falling barometers made itself felt as the convoy slowly formed up into the four columns with Vice-Commodore on *Calobre* heading the first column, *Daldorch* leading the second, the Commodore on *Empire Archer* at the head of the third, and the Rear-Commodore's *Jefferson Myers* leading the fourth. This was the formation it was hoped the convoy would keep all the way to its Russian destination. It was wise because at the head of each column was an experienced master who could be relied upon to lead his column in any movement called for by the Commodore; but it had the disadvantage that the German U-boats knew of these arrangements from their experience in hitting Atlantic convoys, and usually made a dead set at the leading ships in the hope of disrupting the leadership, thus disposing of controlling commodores and deputies.

Nobody felt at all happy. Despite the security-bound life they were living, the seamen had heard stories, both in this country and in America, of the decimation of PQ17 and the beating given to PQ18. The survivors of the former had quite understandably related, with deep bitterness, their conception of what had happened the previous summer. In their eyes the Navy had pulled out under threat of surface action from large German ships, leaving the convoy to the mercy of U-boats and incessant air attacks until only a third of the convoy struggled through. . . . On 25 December, while the first half, JW51A, was arriving incredulously unscathed in Russia, the second part, JW51B, was making its rendezvous with the destroyers under Captain Sherbrooke about 150 miles east of Iceland. There the three Hunt-class destroyers, *Blankney*, *Chiddingfold* and *Ledbury*, and the *Circe* bade them farewell while *Bramble*, *Hyderabad*, *Rhododendron*, *Northern Gem* and *Vizalma* took up their stations as close escort with the destroyers. For the next week or two those gale-lashed, barren seas were to be comparatively heavily populated, because in addition to convoy JW51B with its strong escort, there were also the two cruisers, *Sheffield* and *Jamaica*, with Rear-Admiral Robert L. Burnett and his staff on board *Sheffield* as Force R (including the two destroyers *Opportune* and *Matchless*), the homeward-bound convoy RA52 which sailed on 27 December for Iceland, and (covering the area farther south-west) were heavy units of the Home Fleet—the battleship *Anson*, the cruiser *Cumberland* and the destroyers *Forester* and *Impulsive*.

On paper this looks impressive. There were five or six days when the two convoys JW51B and RA52 would first be nearing, passing, and then leaving each other astern so that with their own escorts and the heavier units in the comparative vicinity it would seem that should an enemy force dare to attempt an attack he would assuredly inherit something of a metaphorical thick ear. But once the variety of factors begin to appear, so too do the complications. To begin with, the weather became progressively more foul. The sun, appearing only for a couple of hours or so on the best days, was otherwise not seen at all. A savage gale, prolonged over days, hammered at the cruisers *Sheffield* and *Jamaica* so they had to sail by dead reckoning, intelligent guesswork. Admiral Burnett had to estimate how far off its designated course JW51B had been blown, and also in what direction in relation to his own estimated course. If he were too far away from the convoy, and it was attacked, by the time he reached the spot it would be only sorrowfully to pick up the remnants. If on the other hand he were too close, and a patrolling submarine spotted him, his usefulness would be diminished. The element of surprise would be wrested from him and he might even find himself fighting for his life against a heavy German unit.

Sheffield and *Jamaica*, each of 9,000 tons and capable of more than thirty knots, slammed north-west, fighting against a succession of awe-inspiring seas which forced them down to ten knots. There were swirling snowstorms and sheets of driving spray which froze as it landed on deck, sheathing the ships in feet-thick layers of ice so that keeping the gun-turrets movable was a major task. By 29-30 December Admiral Burnett estimated that he was south-west of JW51B by around fifty to sixty miles, and was south of Bear Island. In other words according to this estimate he was then between the convoy and the German base at Altenfiord. *Jamaica*, *Sheffield* and the two destroyers were in the danger zone, watching, waiting and—guessing. Coastal Command had been urged by C-in-C Home Fleet to try to keep an eye on the German ships there, but the same foul weather which was providing some measure of protection to JW51B, and making life difficult for Force R, also prevented the RAF from carrying out any look-see flights. The 30th of December saw a cessation of the gales and *Sheffield* was at least able to establish her own position so, if there came a call for help from JW51B, she would have a starting-point.

Admiral Burnett was told by the Admiralty that there was a strong possibility that a German submarine had spotted JW51B as it was passing Bear Island and had reported its position, speed and course. The stage was set. The Germans, still triumphant over their successes against PQ17 and PQ18, could be relied upon to attempt something spectacular, most probably a surface attack with air support. All *Sheffield* and *Jamaica* could do was patrol and wait, ready to make an entry on cue. The main actors in the piece and the reason for *Sheffield* and *Jamaica* being in their present extremely uncomfortable position—namely, the ships of JW51B and their escort—were meanwhile plugging along at around seven knots and entering that vicious area in which they would be much too close to German bases.

JW51B's full escort of destroyers should have been seven, *Onslow* (senior ship), *Oribi*, *Obedient*, *Obdurate* and *Orwell* with *Achates* and *Bulldog*. In the event of an attack the principal task of *Bulldog* and *Achates* would be to make smoke to enable the convoy to turn away while the remainder of the destroyers, under Captain Sherbrooke, endeavoured to deal with the raiders. But on the trip from the Clyde to Seidisford, *Achates* and *Bulldog* ran into extremely bad weather. *Bull-*

dog, after being forced to lie hove-to in an extremely bad gale, was so seriously damaged that sailing her with JW51B was out of the question. *Achates*, too, sprang her topmast, but this was repaired at Seidisford. *Achates* was a disillusioned veteran of the Murmansk run, and northern waters in general. A year previously she had had her bow blown off by a mine off Iceland, and after a long refit did a great deal of convoy and escort work attached to the Clyde Special Escort. In May she had formed part of the escort to PQ16 and was under almost continuous air attack on that trip. She returned with a QP convoy, had a short boiler-cleaning leave and re-emerged in time to be escort to PQ18. On her return she was one of the Home Fleet ships which were sent to Gibraltar, and took part in bombardments and patrols during the North African landings, during which short campaign she was credited with the sinking of an enemy submarine. Returning to the Clyde, *Achates* was escorting the troopship *Warwick Castle* when that ship was torpedoed in a rising gale in the Bay of Biscay. . . .

By the time therefore that *Achates* was in position off JW51B's port bow, her crew had gathered a wealth of experience, had seen many men die. To them, young men, death was something that happened to old relatives—or to other men. The first two or three days—and nights—at sea were always an anxious time for merchant ships and escorts. It must be remembered that there were no steaming lights, and in the long hours of darkness shadows took on a menacing solidity. A cresting wave off the bow would in imagination be the wake of the ship ahead, seemingly much too close; a similar cresting wave, flashing white, close on the beam could be the bow wave of another ship. . . . Escorts, feeling that they had strayed too far from the convoy, would come nudging in until they could see the blacker, vague outlines of the ships, when they would move outwards again.

At stated intervals clocks would buzz on ships denoting the time for an alteration of course to conform with the zigzag agreed between Senior Officer Escort and Commodore. But there was always a chance that a ship would make her turn too late, or use a little too much or too little helm. Nerve-racking. And it was to go on day and night for another ten days before they reached the precarious safety of the White Sea. But JW51B sailed steadily onwards, making good a north-easterly course until on 29 December, by now well inside the Arctic circle, seventy-three degrees north, with the weather breaking down to northerly gales, when course was altered to east. But each turn of a propeller, every minute steamed, increased the danger. The convoy was nearing that tip of Norway where waited German surface ships.

Narvik was little more than 400 miles away, fifteen hours' steaming for a German heavy surface craft. A little farther north and east was Altenfiord, crouching under the hump of North Cape. From there, in order to cut the convoy route, the German ships would have to steam fewer than 200 miles; and if things went wrong with an attack they could bolt for home again in a matter of a few hours.

Truly, JW51B was sailing through the gates of hell.

Thirteen

WHAT were the forces the Germans had available in that area? Apart from submarines, what could they launch against us? On the very day that JW51B sailed from Loch Ewe, 22 December, Admiral Raeder was able to report to Hitler that at Altenfiord he had ready for sea the heavy cruiser *Admiral Hipper*, the pocket-battleship *Lützow*, the cruiser *Köln* and five destroyers. At Narvik were the cruiser *Nürnberg* and two destroyers, and at Trondhjem were the *Tirpitz* with three destroyers. After their recent successes the jubilant Germans were entitled to assume that they had this northern convoy to Russia business neatly lined-up for future slaughter.

From September, when PQ18 was attacked, they kept up unceasing U-boat patrols across all the probable courses a convoy might take. Day and night the U-boats reported 'nothing doing'. Through October and into the foul weather of November and December it had been the same. But the German Naval Staff prepared a plan to attack any convoy which had the temerity to attempt the passage. They knew, of course, that no matter what course a convoy steered, ultimately it would have to pass close to that lethal tip of north Norway. For just that occasion a plan was prepared.

Operation Rainbow (*Regenbogen*), with an alternative plan, Operation Aurora. Rainbow provided for *Hipper*, *Lützow* and several destroyers to sail from Altenfiord to attack. Aurora provided for the *Lützow* to sail alone, commerce-raiding, or to sail with *Hipper*, hit the convoy and then go off on a raiding mission into the Atlantic.

The surface units available to the Germans were terrifyingly heavy. The *Hipper* was a heavy cruiser with eight 8-inch guns and twelve 37-mm. anti-aircraft guns. She was capable of doing thirty-two knots. *Lützow*, sister-ship to the *Admiral Graf Spee*, which we had fought and forced to scuttle herself in 1939, had six 11-inch guns, firing a shell weighing 670 lb. over a range of fifteen miles. She could steam at twenty-six knots. *Lützow* (originally named *Deutschland*) had been launched in 1931. Both *Hipper* and *Lützow* had nothing to fear from the British destroyers escorting JW51B, armed as they were with 4.7 or 4-inch guns. Even the six German destroyers had either four or five 5-inch guns and could steam at thirty-six knots.

The Germans actually sighted JW51A, reported rather vaguely by a patrolling U-boat; but it was too far east to implement Operation Rainbow and was therefore not attacked. But there was prompt reaction when JW51B was reported by Lieutenant Herschleb in U-354. This the Germans, unaware of the change of convoy destination, called PQ20 and preparations were made for an attack. Herschleb, reporting from U-354, had given an optimistic estimate of the speed of the convoy. He had reported it was steaming east at twelve knots, nearly four knots faster than it was actually sailing. The German Staff, poring over large charts, estimated where JW51B would be at a certain time and based the attack on that estimate.

Admiral Hipper, flagship of Admiral Kummetz, *Lützow*, and six destroyers were brought to immediate notice for steam, the channel from Altenfiord was carefully swept for mines while the Germans held a short conference on *Hipper*. She was commanded by Captain Hans Hartmann and *Lützow* by Captain Stang. Kummetz outlined his plan of battle: *Hipper* and three destroyers would be one force, and *Lützow* and the other three destroyers would constitute the other. They would separate and attack the convoy from different directions. The ships sailed as one force from Altenfiord, then split. *Hipper* was accompanied by the destroyers *Friedrich Eckholdt*, *Richard Beitzen* and Z29, and *Lützow* by destroyers Z30, Z31 and *Theodor Riedel*. Once in the open sea in darkness they parted. Either force, at any rate on paper, was capable of decimating the convoy and their escort and—at a pinch—also dealing with *Sheffield* and *Jamaica*.

Submarines U-354 and U-626 were in the meantime hanging on to the convoy, transmitting frequent reports of speed and course. Kummetz's plan was to place *Lützow* and her three destroyers seventy-five miles south of *Hipper* at 1800 hours that evening. Both ships would station their destroyers fifteen miles apart and fifteen miles ahead, and would then search eastwards along the convoy's course. This meant that the Germans would have a searching screen seventy-odd miles wide. With the help of the U-boats Kummetz hoped to locate the convoy just before dawn which would give him time to concentrate his forces on their task of destruction in the few short hours of daylight.

The plan of attack, assuming the German forces met the convoy where it expected to do so, was for *Hipper* and her destroyers to attack one side of the convoy, draw off the escorting forces, engage them, destroy them, then hit the unprotected assembly of merchant ships with *Lützow* and her consorts. Finally, both groups were to converge for the eventual kill.

A curious point arises here. A signal, made to Kummetz by Admiral Kluger, C-in-C German Naval Forces in north Norway, illustrates the extreme caution imposed on Kummetz. Part of the signal read: '. . . Avoid a superior force, otherwise destroy according to tactical situation. . . .' What exactly was Kummetz to regard as a 'superior force'? The Germans had a number of submarines patrolling near Bear Island besides some more hanging on to the convoy, so it was at least an even chance that they would spot and report any heavy British forces giving the convoy close support.

Two or three resolutely handled destroyers, attacking in poor visibility, thrusting home their attacks to fire torpedoes at a heavy cruiser or pocket-battleship would constitute a threat, but could scarcely be called a 'superior force', neither could *Sheffield* and *Jamaica* be so designated. So anxious was Admiral Kluger that *Hipper* and *Lützow* should not become embroiled in a stand-up fight that another signal read: 'Contrary to the operational order regarding contact against the enemy use caution *even against enemy of equal strength* because it is undesirable for the cruisers to take any great risks.' (The italics are mine—E. B.)

So after a carefully planned operation against a convoy, an operation designed to destroy it after disposing of its escort, Kummetz was sent to sea and was later cautioned to be extremely careful. There has never been any evidence produced to show that the German admirals were cowards, or afraid of action. Witness the destruction of *Bismarck*. She fought to the last when it was realized that the fate of a marauder had overtaken her. The trouble was that if *Hipper* and/or *Lützow* were sunk or damaged for the price of part of a convoy, Hitler would indulge in one of his periodic rages against the navy. The spectacular successes against earlier convoys had been achieved by a combination of U-boats and aircraft, not heavy surface craft.

So dawned 31 December, the last day of the year, with JW51B steaming on an easterly course at around nine knots, and closing in on it was an enemy force. At 0730 hours *Hipper* detected some vague silhouettes bearing 090 degrees and sent destroyers to investigate. The British escorting force was expecting some Russian destroyers to join up with them—actually this was an error due to a distorted signal. The original message from Senior Naval Officer North Russia had said Russian aircraft would join the convoy. So when in her turn *Hyderabad* sighted the vague outlines of two destroyers south of the convoy, it was assumed that they were the Russians and the Intelligence was not reported immediately to *Onslow*.

A few minutes later *Obdurate*, also on the starboard or south side of the convoy, sighted two destroyers south of her. *Obdurate*'s captain knew of the possibility of the Russian destroyers joining the convoy and sent by signal lamp a signal to *Onslow*, via *Obedient*, reporting the presence of the two strangers. *Obdurate* was sent off to make contact and establish the identity of the destroyers. She swung away from her position on the starboard beam of the convoy and closed the strangers. Visibility and light were bad, but *Obdurate* was able to determine that there were three, not two, destroyers and that they were steaming north across the wake of the convoy.

Obdurate challenged but got no reply. Instead, the three strangers turned away and steamed westward for a while then swung on a northerly course. Once again *Obdurate*, having increased speed, challenged while her bridge personnel peered through binoculars trying to establish from the hazy outlines sufficient to enable identification. Instead of replying to the challenge, one of the destroyers opened fire on *Obdurate*. The first shells of the Battle of the Barents Sea had been fired.

The British destroyers knew what they had to do. The fleet destroyers, *Onslow*, *Obedient*, *Orwell* and *Obdurate*, would fight under Captain Sherbrooke's direction; the *Achates* would remain with the convoy, making smoke as required, and the other escort ships would remain closed up with the convoy. *Onslow* and *Orwell* tore across the head of the convoy on a north-westerly course, with *Obedient* swinging around its stern, racing to join *Onslow* and *Orwell*. Meanwhile the three German destroyers had turned off on a northerly course and *Obdurate*, having established that they were enemy craft, steered to join her leader. On *Onslow*'s bridge they were peering through the murk. A snow-squall descended on the ships, blotting out everything for a while. As it cleared *Onslow* sighted the bulk of a ship on her starboard bow. This loomed out of the snow, obviously something larger than a destroyer. The radio began to chatter on the Fleet wavelength reporting this new menace. For a few minutes they thought there was a possibility that the larger ship looming out of the murk was either *Sheffield* or *Jamaica*, Force R.

But doubts were set at rest when the three German destroyers, one of which had fired at *Obdurate*, were seen joining the large ship, which was *Hipper*. The four British destroyers were racing northwards to meet a German cruiser and three destroyers, at least. So far as they knew to the contrary there might be more German ships hidden in the murk. The Commodore of the convoy knew his part. He ordered an emergency turn to the south as *Achates* positioned herself on the port wing of the convoy to use the north-westerly wind to blow her smoke to cover the convoy. *Hyderabad*, *Rhododendron* and *Northern Gem* also moved to make smoke between the enemy and the turning convoy.

The German force and the British destroyers were by now converging on each other at a mean speed of more than sixty miles an hour, in visibility occasionally cut down to a couple of miles, but which sometimes lengthened as the squalls passed. As yet there had been no firing except for the one broadside fired at *Obdurate*. Visibility, bad as it was most of the time, was a help to the British force of destroyers. For *Hipper* and her consorts to fulfil their task of destroying the convoy, they would have to close in on it. They could not stand off at extreme range and shell with impunity. And as yet *Hipper* could not see the convoy; against the lighter sky to the south she could see a thickening of the haze which was the smoke-screen being made by *Achates*.

She was to be *Hipper*'s first target. Shortly after 0930 *Hipper* fired her first broadside, four turrets, two for'ard, two aft. The salvo of eight shells surrounded the destroyer—for a few moments she disappeared behind the towering columns of water, then she emerged still making the thin black line of smoke which rapidly expanded into an opaque screen. *Hipper* was shooting at six miles' range. Another and yet another salvo bracketed *Achates*, and again she emerged, at last hit, limping, but still making smoke. Then *Hipper*, for some reason, switched her fire to a laggard tanker steaming behind the convoy, the *Empire Emerald*, firing two salvos at her without damaging her, then she switched once more to *Achates*.

Onslow, *Obedient* and *Orwell*, steering a north-easterly course, were firing as hard as they could at *Hipper*. It was not to be expected that their 4.7 and 4-inch guns would do her any material damage—the shells would scarcely dent her armour—but there was a profound uplifting effect of the guns blazing away, and if *Hipper* continued on her present course there was a chance that the destroyers would be able to fire their torpedoes at her. This real threat to *Hipper* was always there; in fact, by not firing torpedoes, but by merely getting into a position to do so, *Onslow*, *Orwell* and *Obedient* were acting as would the snapping sheep-dogs looking after a flock. Those snarling rushes might at any time develop from a feint into a real attack. *Hipper* finally turned north behind a smoke-screen.

Captain Sherbrooke had another worry. *Hipper* had been

doing an almost classic move by drawing away the escort, and the absence of the three German destroyers from the scene made him wonder if they had turned south and east to attack the convoy from its starboard side. He therefore ordered *Obedient* and *Obdurate* to rejoin the convoy, still steering south-east behind the smoke-screen. And at that moment there came a signal from *Sheffield*: 'Am approaching you on a course of 170 degrees.' So Force R, *Sheffield* and *Jamaica*, were north of the convoy, north of Sherbrooke's force, and north of *Hipper*. But how far north? His navigating officer's estimate was anywhere between thirty and a hundred and thirty miles.

JW51B had been blown south of its course by the three days' gale, there had been no chance of taking accurate sights—it was all guesswork. As we have seen, *Sheffield* and *Jamaica*, also working on guesswork dead-reckoning, were north of the convoy instead of being south of it. And half an hour's resolute work by *Hipper* could dispose of the escorting British destroyers, leaving her a clear field in which to destroy the convoy.

Captain Sherbrooke sadly missed his other destroyer *Oribi*, the other smoke-maker, *Bulldog* and *Bramble* and the trawler *Vizalma*—about which more later. *Achates* and *Bulldog* could possibly have put up a show against the three absent German destroyers, and *Bramble* and the trawler could have intensified the smoke-screen. The earlier part of this action had been fought in intense cold, with the driving spray and snow-squalls falling on the ships and freezing as it fell. Occasionally visibility was down to less than a mile. For the moment Sherbrooke was satisfied. A large German unit had attacked the convoy he was guarding, and by his tactics he had compelled the enemy force to withdraw to the north-west while his convoy steamed south-east behind a smoke-screen.

First round to Sherbrooke. But, it was only the first round.

Now Sherbrooke's worry was to keep his depleted force of destroyers between the known enemy, *Hipper*, and the convoy, and at the same time be prepared for an onslaught by another part of the enemy unit. But where was it? Where were the three destroyers which had opened fire at *Obdurate*, thus beginning the action? Sherbrooke turned east to steam parallel with the original convoy course, so that he was in a position to launch another feint at *Hipper* if she reappeared from the north-west, or he could swing into action south-east if a new threat developed.

We will for a moment leave JW51B steaming safely south-east and go back three days . . . for those days have a bearing on subsequent events. Had JW51B not been blown south of its course, *Hipper*, *Lützow* and the destroyers might not have met it where they did. In fact there would have been a possibility that the shadowing U-boats would have sighted Force R, *Sheffield* and *Jamaica*, and a battle-royal of big ships would have followed on the lines of the Battle of the River Plate, with the odds heavily against the two British cruisers.

So back to 28 December.

Fourteen

THE convoy, six days out from Loch Ewe, had settled down into a compact mass of shipping. Ships had begun to assess one another; there were no stragglers, and the escorts were in position around it. Then the weather smote it. In the late hours of the 28th and the morning of the 29th a real Arctic gale developed. Mountainous seas, their crests being whipped off by the wind hammered at the ships, escorts and convoy and heavy snow-squalls blotted out everything until it seemed that each ship was steaming along in a white hell of its own.

Around midnight the Rear-Commodore's ship, the American *Jefferson Myers*, rolling heavily, signalled that the heavy crates containing bombers lashed to her deck were beginning to break adrift. She said that she could not maintain her course and speed. *Jefferson Myers* pulled away from the convoy and lay hove-to, not taking so much punishment, as her crew fought to secure the unwieldy crates. Soon she was alone in that vast Arctic waste, and no longer resembled a ship so much as a gigantic iced cake with ice feet thick all over her.

At the same time a garbled low-power signal was received from the destroyer *Oribi*—apparently she had lost the convoy because of a gyro compass failure. For a brief interval during the night she rejoined, but again lost the convoy. It must have been a harrowing, nerve-racking night on *Oribi's* bridge. Without her gyro compass and with nothing to help her she could have been steaming blind north-west, south-west or even south, heading for a collision through an opaque, driving snowstorm. At daylight, completely alone, *Oribi* searched for the convoy for twenty-four hours and, using a very inaccurate boat compass, steamed for Kola Inlet independently, arriving on 31 December at roughly the time *Hipper* was endeavouring to destroy the convoy.

A savage gale, raging down from the Polar regions, was playing havoc with JW51B. The waves were twenty feet high, roaring along at forty miles an hour and hitting the ships and slamming over them in sheets of white spray which froze almost as soon as it touched the decks and upperworks. *Daldorch* signalled that her deck cargo had carried away and she would have to alter course and heave-to until the weather eased. Sending these signals by a winking light was not easy: a signalman would be slashed by a shower of needle-like spray or would try to face up to a flurry of biting snow, while his opposite number on the Commodore ship would be reading snatches of signal with streaming eyes. So the confusion which arose was completely pardonable. When *Daldorch* pulled away from her position in the inner port column, the ships in the outer port column veered away from her also swinging to port. For a while there were ships steaming at all angles and all courses, and for two hours it was confusion. Around 0200 hours the trawler *Vizalma*, bucking and pitching, most of the time under solid water, established that she and three merchant ships were on their own. They were the *Calobre,* Vice-Commodore of the convoy, *Chester Valley* and *Daldorch,* with the *Jefferson Myers* still taking a savage beating not far away.

The four ships and the trawler lay hove-to, all steering different courses according to how the masters found them most at ease. *Vizalma* nudged up close to *Chester Valley* and stayed near her until noon when the weather moderated, and on 30 December the ships began to move east again towards their destination. But they were no longer a convoy of fourteen ships; neither had they an escort capable of fighting. Gun-breeches were frozen solid, sheets of ice joined gun-barrels to the decks, depth-charges were solid in the racks and torpedoes were locked in their tubes. The one consolation was that if an enemy force was in the neighbourhood—at least, surface craft—they would be in a similar useless condition.

The problem facing Sherbrooke was twofold. The precious convoy was reduced by a third, only nine ships could be shepherded once more into formation, and he was short of two escort ships, *Oribi* and *Vizalma.* How far south the convoy had been driven was anybody's guess, for the ships had been steering all courses during the gale. It could indeed be anything from forty to seventy miles south of the original route. All hands available were put to the task of smashing ice from every form of armament so as to make them as effective as quickly as possible.

The convoy speed was set at six knots so as to give the stragglers a chance to re-join. This could be maintained for only a short while, for otherwise it would complicate the schedule which was arranged for *Sheffield* and *Jamaica* to be in position to guard the convoy at the critical stage when it was close to the German bases. At first daylight on the 30th—it was merely a lightening of the opaque grey—the first of the missing ships caught up and took her position in the convoy. Sherbrooke then decided to send *Bramble* in search of the others as she was fitted with the latest type of search radar. She thereupon swung away to the north-west —but was never seen again by British eyes.

An hour later, just when the Commodore decided to increase the speed of the convoy, there appeared—plunging up from the south-west, bows smashing into the sea and throwing back sheets of spray—two more of the stragglers. Only now missing were *Oribi*, *Chester Valley* and the faithful trawler *Vizalma*. But as soon as the weather had moderated the trawler and merchant ship slammed along at eleven knots and actually passed ahead of the convoy (north of it) without spotting it. Through the murk *Vizalma* did see some signal-lights flashing, but wisely decided to ignore them as they might have been German surface craft. Actually *Vizalma* and her precious charge *Chester Valley* arrived quite safely in Russia, passing north of the battle between Sherbrooke's destroyers, later the cruisers, and the German forces. So once again the convoy, virtually intact, sailed nearer at every turn of their screws to the danger zone which lay off the tip of Norway.

Captain Sherbrooke was warned, around noon on 30 December, that there was a great deal of German radio activity in north Norway. It could be anything; possibly the convoy had been sighted and reported (as it had by U-boats), or the presence of the big ships, *Anson, Cumberland* and destroyers, had sparked off an alarm, or maybe Force R, *Sheffield* and *Jamaica*, had been reported. Of one thing Captain Sherbrooke, however, was certain. Tomorrow his ships and the convoy would be in the vital zone—less than 200 miles from Altenfiord—and if German surface ships were abroad, their primary objective would be the destruction of JW51B, destroying him and his force with it. And his task was to prevent that at all costs—no provisions had been made for him to be cautious in face of a superior force, or even one of equal force. For him it would mean fighting to the last ship and man in defence of JW51B. There was to be no repetition of PQ17.

Through the fleeting hours of 30 December the weary men on the destroyers hammered and smashed at the ice covering their ships until by nightfall they were reasonably fighting efficient. Only the men, exhausted after the indescribable weather, were nearing the limits of their endurance. . . . Mercifully they were not to know that next day they would be called upon to draw even deeper upon their waning resources. . . . *Bramble*, still searching for the lame ducks, was north of the convoy, ploughing her lonely way, straining eyes watching the radar screen for the flicker of green-white which would show her that she had made a contact. The early afternoon semi-darkness slowly drifted into the opaque blackness of night, and gradually the Old Year passed away.

The three days' gale had left men exhausted. Gun-crews slept where and how they could, crouched together in groups for a little warmth and comfort, stretched out on ammunition lockers, scarcely believing that life could produce such torture. The middle watch, midnight to four o'clock, passed with dragging minutes which seemed hours long, hours which were as wearisome as days. Then came the morning watch, with a perceptible lightening of the sky to the south. . . .

Hipper had by now detected the vague outlines of ships and was shadowing them, while her attendant destroyers investigated closer. *Hyderabad*'s starboard look-out, peering from cold-punished eyes just after 0800 hours, observed two destroyers almost due south of her, but committed the unpardonable offence of assuming that they were friendly. She made no challenge, neither did she report their presence to *Onslow*, or at least to the nearest British destroyers. Even had they been Russian, one would have assumed that *Hyderabad* would have attempted to establish that fact, and then report to the Senior Ship that his escort force was being strengthened by the addition of the Russian destroyers. Some minutes later a look-out on *Obdurate* sighted the two destroyers still south of the convoy, but rather more astern. They were in fact crossing the convoy's course from south-east to north-west. *Obdurate*, fully aware that—according to the garbled signal—some Russian destroyers might be joining, also assumed that the two newcomers were friendly and accordingly sent a message to *Onslow* by signal-lamp via *Obedient*. That was done at 0830 hours. For the signal to pass from ship to ship took time and it was nearly 0850 hours by the time it reached *Onslow*, and a similar lapse of time for another signal to return to *Obdurate* via *Obedient.* All this lamp chatter about Russian destroyers must have made *Obedient's* bridge personnel rather touchy. And understandably too. Somewhere south and astern of her were a couple of mysterious destroyers which people right, left and centre were assuming to be friendly. Nobody on *Obedient's* bridge could see them in the half-darkness, so *Obedient* went to 'Action Stations', acting on the sound principle 'Let friends reveal themselves, but if they are not friends then I'm ready!'

Obdurate, as we have seen earlier, closed the strangers, challenged but received no reply. Now this non-acknowledgement was not unusual, for Russian ships were prone to take their time about answering challenges. Then *Obdurate* was fired on.

The first phase of the battle to protect the convoy had gone much as Sherbrooke had visualized. Like all commanding officers and senior officers of escorts he must have gone over in his mind a hundred times exactly what he would do in the event of his charge—the convoy—being attacked. He must have visualized an infinite variety of attacks from a penny-plain-tuppence-coloured all-out attack by aircraft as well as an attack by 'wolf-packs' of submarines, to an attempt by heavy surface craft. Against these various possible forms of assault he had prepared his defence, some of which he had committed to paper for the information of the other ships, but the rest he had carried in his mind.

Of one thing he was dogmatically certain; that until the last escort ship was sunk the convoy would not be defenceless, and that last ship would be destroyed fighting between it and the merchant ships. The attack which had materialized up to now was identified as being made by a heavy surface craft and destroyers, and he had beaten it off, not by any weight of gunfire but by a sustained threat of torpedo action pushed to the ultimate, even to the point of emulating little *Glowworm* which had rammed a German heavy ship in her last moments of life. Sherbrooke harboured no delusions: this was not the end of the fight. When *Hipper* turned away to the North it was the end of a round. His force was intact; so was *Hipper's*. And he was as certain that another attack would come as he was that in whatever form it came he would meet it.

After the war, when German records were made available to us, it was possible to fit in missing pieces of this Devil's Dance in the Arctic. Admiral Kummetz wrote of Sherbrooke's first counter-attack:

'The British destroyers conducted themselves very skilfully. They placed themselves in such a position between *Hipper* and the convoy that it was impossible to get near the ships. They made very effective use of a smoke-screen with which to hide the merchant ships. They dodged *Hipper's* fire by taking avoiding action and using smoke. They forced *Hipper* to run the risk of a torpedo attack while trying to use her guns on the merchant ships.'

In that passage is a true valediction to little *Achates*, steaming steadily along a course, firing no guns, but making smoke. Even later, when a battered wreck and sinking, she still made smoke 'to hide the merchant ships'. Kummetz, of course, knew something which Sherbrooke only feared. South of the convoy, and converging on it, was *Lützow* and her attendant destroyers. To her, Kummetz signalled that he was in action against the convoy and that there were four destroyers between him and the merchant ships. This was a slight exaggeration. Actually against him at that moment he had *Onslow* and *Orwell*.

Kummetz had failed in his attempt to draw Sherbrooke and his force farther north, so shortly after 1000 hours he turned south-east again. For five minutes or more she blazed away at the two destroyers which were between her and the convoy, but they twisted and weaved to dodge his fire, resolutely refusing to be driven from their task. Until those destroyers were sunk, or forced to turn away, *Hipper* was unable to get at the convoy. And they refused to turn. Meanwhile *Obedient* and *Obdurate* were steaming down towards the convoy, making smoke; and *Achates*, badly hit, was still obstinately carrying out her task. Eventually Kummetz decided to bring the full weight of his armament to bear on *Onslow* and *Orwell*. In addition to this formidable fire, his three destroyers, close astern of *Hipper*, were also blazing away.

The outcome was inevitable. *Hipper*, firing rapid broadsides at *Onslow* and *Orwell*, arrived at the correct range and deluged the destroyers. In reply *Onslow* could only bring to bear two guns, because the other two were jammed with ice. Salvo after salvo from the German ships burst close alongside the ships, splinters cutting through *Onslow's* thin plates. Then *Onslow* was hit again and again. Captain Sherbrooke was severely wounded in the face, his ship was on fire in several places, and dead and dying men lay all over the ship. In less than two minutes nearly fifty of her crew were killed or wounded.

Astern of her was *Orwell*. From *Orwell's* bridge they saw *Onslow* hit and reel away, vicious dark-red flames and black smoke rolling from her. *Orwell* raced up to place herself between the stricken *Onslow* and *Hipper* and began to make a smoke-screen to cover her. This made *Orwell* the main target, and on her commanding officer, Lieutenant-Commander N. H. G. Austen, rested the weight of heavy decision. Should he turn his ship and make a desperate all-out attack on *Hipper* in the hope of hitting her with torpedoes? It would probably, even undoubtedly, mean his destruction and would still leave the German ship able to dispose of *Onslow* then close in on the convoy.

In the meantime *Obedient*, in response to a signal from *Onslow*, was racing back to join her crippled leader. And then the shooting stopped. To Lieutenant-Commander Austen's astonishment *Hipper* turned away to the north, ceased firing and disappeared out of sight into a snow-squall. Captain Sherbrooke, his face smashed and practically blind, had been prevailed upon to go below to his room where he was given attention. He still issued orders and instructed that a signal be made to *Obedient*, next in seniority and therefore senior fighting ship now that he was retiring on the convoy: 'Making smoke-screen'.

Crippled, her guns out of action, fires raging in several places and her captain severely wounded, *Onslow* was still concentrating on the main task of giving the convoy every possible chance of escaping until Force R arrived to redress the balance. Indeed, as she steered south towards the convoy, *Onslow* added that she also intended to home Force R on the convoy. In the middle of this battle, about the time that *Onslow* was being battered, a brief signal was received from the lonely *Bramble* that she had sighted a cruiser.

After hammering *Onslow*, *Hipper* inexplicably turned away to the north-east. She emerged from the snow-squall and sighted what a look-out reported to be a destroyer to north of her. It was this ship's presence which probably disturbed *Hipper* in her destruction of *Onslow* and *Orwell*. Another ship, especially a destroyer to north of him, made him the meat in the sandwich. *Hipper* turned north and engaged this new 'threat'. *Bramble* was a ship of 800 tons, a minesweeper being used as an escort, manned by seven officers and 113 ratings, and armed with one 4-inch gun. *Hipper* hammered her for six minutes, during which time Commander Rust, her commanding officer, managed to get away the short signal which *Hyderabad* had received. *Hipper* left *Bramble* a shambles, barely afloat, a charnel house, and turned south again once more to attack the convoy. But *Bramble* had not died in vain.

The threat from the 'destroyer' on his port side, to his north, had made Kummetz turn away from destroying *Onslow*, then *Orwell* which was moving in to take over the convoy. Kummetz knew, of course, that somewhere south or south-west of the convoy *Lützow* and her destroyers were racing in for the kill. Quite confidently he expected to hear at any time that this lean, dark wolf had crashed into the convoy which was fleeing south-east, and was decimating it. It was something that the British force, now commanded by

Commander Kinloch in *Obedient*, had to fear. There was no certain information that another enemy force was operating with *Hipper*, or where it was operating, but the overworked, harassed destroyers had to be prepared to meet it. But they did know that somewhere in the vicinity was Force R, *Sheffield* and *Jamaica*.

The alert little corvette *Rhododendron* on the port quarter of the convoy first saw smoke ahead and reported it to *Obedient*. While this disturbing item of information was being digested, *Rhododendron* came up again with another signal to the effect that she had sighted an unknown warship two miles away which was steering roughly north. The stranger (actually it was *Lützow*) did not open fire for some reason, although it was crossing the bows of the convoy at only 4,000 yards. *Hyderabad* also sighted two destroyers, as well as—a few minutes later—a larger ship, crossing the convoy's path; but made no report.

Lützow had actually sighted some of the ships in the van of the convoy before the German destroyers began the action by firing at *Obdurate*. Captain Stang decided that he would shadow it for a while, then saw gun-flashes to his north. Reasonably he supposed that *Hipper* and her destroyers were already beginning their slaughter. He would continue on his present course, and in due time the fleeing remnants of the convoy, turning from *Hipper*, would drop into his lap. *Hipper's* later signal confirmed him in this decision, so for nearly an hour he steamed slowly northeast, waiting.

All this action was not fought out in clear air. There were vicious snow-squalls, the light was of no more value than late afternoon in mid-winter and the cloud base was 'down on the waves'. Ships loomed up out of the squalls and were sharply defined for a few seconds, then disappeared again. It was like peering through binoculars with the adjustment being rapidly and extensively varied. *Lützow's* decision to steam slowly and wait lost him a glorious opportunity. Apart from the crippled *Onslow* and badly damaged *Achates* still faithfully making a smoke-screen, there were three destroyers, *Obedient*, *Orwell* and *Obdurate*, and three smaller ships, the sphinx-like *Hyderabad* and the tiny but alert corvette *Rhododendron* and *Northern Gem* facing him. Of this pathetically small force the three destroyers were still obstinately placing themselves between *Hipper* and the convoy.

Lützow had six 11-inch guns, eight 5.9-inch guns, six 4.1-inch guns, besides three destroyers each armed with four 5-inch guns, yet her captain (Stang) steamed this terrifying quantity of armament three miles away from the convoy for nearly an hour and did not fire one shot! His orders were to be cautious even in the face of equal force. Stang *was* cautious. The irony of the situation was that *Hipper*, despite the fact that she failed to thrust home her first attacks—that same over-riding caution—had nevertheless completed the first part of Operation Rainbow to perfection. The convoy had been located, the escorts had been attacked and drawn off to the north side of the convoy. *Lützow* was ideally placed to complete the task. They could, and should, have been steaming home by midday with chests proudly inflated for the Iron Crosses, leaving behind them a holocaust of stricken ships—a sea littered with wreckage and an appalling story of death and destruction. Instead, the convoy, still keeping perfect station and sheltering behind smoke, steamed south-east.

The position at approximately 1100 hours on this bitterly cold, snow-lashed morning was briefly thus: JW51B was steaming south-east in perfect order. To the north and slightly astern of the convoy were the three effective British destroyers, *Obedient*, *Orwell* and *Obdurate*, sore-pressed, trying to be in half a dozen places at the same time, but still full of fight. North of them again was *Hipper* and her three destroyers. South and east of the convoy, steaming at the same speed, was *Lützow* and her three destroyers. And most northerly of all, searching for the convoy and for the enemy, was Force R, *Sheffield* and *Jamaica*.

And the whole Devil's Broth boiling up in an area of approximately the size of Guildford.

Fifteen

HIPPER turned south again shortly after 1100 hours apparently determined to force the pace, and once again she was turned away by little *Bramble*. *Hipper* had left the minesweeper smashed beyond recognition, a smoking shell with more dead men on her than there were live—but she was still afloat. When *Bramble* loomed up, *Hipper* turned towards her and once more attacked, again failing to sink her. Eventually this gory task was left to one of the German destroyers, but the *coup de grâce* had taken time, valuable time, during which Force R was closing in. And closing in it was.

In command was Admiral Burnett, an old hand at this Arctic nightmare. He had commanded the fighting destroyer escort from the cruiser *Scylla*—sixteen destroyers which, as we have seen, fought PQ18 through. Force R, groping in the murk north of JW51B, and its escort were actually nearer than Captain Sherbrooke had imagined. She had picked up on her search radar a couple of contacts to the north of her, shadowed them for a time until it was considered that at the speed they were moving they must be stragglers from the convoy. In fact, they were the trawler *Vizalma* and *Chester Valley*. Between 0930 hours and

1030 hours more radar contacts were made and some gun-flashes were seen in the murk to the south. These actually came from the German destroyers firing at *Obdurate*. The heavier gun-flashes were made by *Hipper* shooting at the convoy and at *Achates*.

Admiral Burnett was confronted with a perplexing problem or, rather, two. The first was: where was the convoy and in what direction was it steaming? Had it been attacked from the south, and made a turn to the north-east? The second was: where were the enemy ships, and in what direction were they steaming? The gun-flashes he had seen could have been made by a detached escort meeting small opposition while rounding up stragglers—an inevitable and unenviable task after a gale such as the one which had recently blown itself out.

A basic in all British naval fighting is 'steam for the sound of the guns', a variation of Nelson's classic order to 'lay alongside an enemy'. But if Admiral Burnett blindly followed that principle would he be chasing after some subsidiary scrap between a couple of destroyers around a detached group of stragglers and thus be moving away from the main fight? Another anxiety for the Admiral was the size of the enemy force. From intelligence, as well as knowledge of what the Germans had available, he might run into *Lützow*, *Hipper*, *Nürnberg*, a flotilla of destroyers, together with a few submarines holding the edge of the ring. In the end Admiral Burnett committed himself to a southerly course at twenty-five knots.

Sheffield and *Jamaica* slammed south towards the area from which were coming the heavier gun-flashes. It was intensely cold—freezing hard, in fact—and had the ships been stationary the cold would have been bone-chilling. Now they were doing twenty-seven knots and on the open bridges of the ships no clothing devised by man could keep the cold out. Eyes were streaming as men peered into the murk. Radar would occasionally show a contact, but then only a spot. . . . Identification would have to be made visually. Astern, her bow wave gleaming in the half-light, *Jamaica* followed *Sheffield*, and as the speed was increased to thirty knots she kept perfect station. Gradually the confused picture ahead began to take shape. There were two battles in progress to the south: one was dead ahead and the other to Burnett's south-east. Were the big Germans among the merchant ships? Were the destroyers fighting for their lives and for the convoy?

Sheffield and *Jamaica* by now had reached the fringes of the slowly dispersing smoke-screen still being made by the crippled *Achates* and *Onslow*. What lay behind the screen? Friend or foe—or both? Radar showed two large contacts ahead, and large contacts moving at the speed they were travelling could only be German surface craft. One was eight or nine miles away, the other was rather more than fifteen miles off. In actual fact they were the *Hipper* and *Lützow*, in that order. *Lützow* had steamed across the bows of the convoy which had made another emergency turn and was now going south, still in good order, still unscathed. *Hipper*, the nearest contact, having paused a few minutes to hammer at the wreck of the *Bramble* (her gun-flashes had been seen by *Sheffield*), now turned to attack the nearest British destroyer, *Obedient*, and also to fire again on the faithful *Achates*.

Suddenly *Hipper* found herself bracketed by salvo after salvo—the first was over, the second was short, but close, the third was slightly off, so too was the fourth. Then a hit. A blast of red, which changed to a dull glow amidships on *Hipper*, showed a hit. That was *Sheffield's* contribution. *Jamaica* followed suit. She was scoring hits on her fourth, fifth and sixth salvos. Force R had arrived and had begun business. And it had achieved complete surprise. *Hipper* was busy firing to one side, hammering at *Obedient*, when *Sheffield* and *Jamaica* hit her from the other side. In less than six minutes *Hipper* had been hit several times. One of her boilers had been damaged, a turbine was out of action, and she was slowed down to just over twenty knots. She also had some fires to contend with.

The British cruisers brought the range down to four miles —a risk this, but one which Burnett was prepared to take. *Hipper* could have hammered both her attackers at eleven miles' range, at which distance neither *Sheffield's* nor *Jamaica's* shell would have been lethal. At four miles a hit could pay a handsome dividend. *Hipper's* attendant destroyers laid a smoke-screen behind which she retired. Now it was guesswork what she intended doing. Was she retreating away to the west, or did she intend to circle completely?

Force R joined in this deadly waltz and pirouetted around as well. Suddenly ahead of them they saw a German destroyer in a perfect position for a torpedo attack. *Sheffield* turned *towards* the destroyer to comb any torpedo attack and if necessary to ram. Seven salvos at less than two miles *Sheffield* poured into the German destroyer *Friedrich Eckholdt*, and as she passed down the side of *Sheffield* even the multiple pom-poms and the 4-inch anti-aircraft guns blazed at her. The *Friedrich Eckholdt*, incidentally, was the destroyer which finally sank intrepid little *Bramble*. Nemesis stalked close behind. Meanwhile *Jamaica* was handing out a belting to a second German destroyer, the *Richard Beitzen*, which, frantically making a smoke-screen, tore off away behind it.

Let us leave Force R for a moment. *Obedient* realized that a bigger brother was now tackling *Hipper*, so taking *Orwell* and *Obdurate* with her, she steamed south to re-assume her primary task—namely, to protect the convoy. This was still steaming south, keeping good order with *Onslow* ahead of it, leaking badly and fighting fires, but still steaming. *Achates*, badly damaged by *Hipper*'s attacks, was slowly sinking, but continued to make the concealing smoke which had been her task all through the action. On the convoy's quarters were *Rhododendron* and the trawler *Northern Gem*. For the time being the convoy was safe, but somewhere ahead was *Lützow* and her destroyers, still intact, still capable of dealing with *Sheffield* and *Jamaica*, and still capable of destroying the convoy. . . . *Lützow*, now to the east of the convoy, had witnessed through the murk the destruction of the German destroyer and had altered course to north-west. She opened fire on the convoy with both her 11-inch guns and secondary armament of 5.9-inch guns without registering a hit. *Obedient*, *Orwell* and *Obdurate* returned the fire, but it was more of a gesture than a threat.

Force R, *Sheffield* and *Jamaica*, hackles up, turned to look for the other heavy German ship. They sighted two German destroyers steaming parallel to them and beyond them the *Lützow*. *Sheffield* and *Jamaica* opened fire accurately and began to close her. Suddenly more shells than *Lützow* was firing straddled them. It was *Hipper*, once more back in the ring. Admiral Burnett now found himself in action against the German pocket-battleship *Lützow*, the heavy cruiser *Hipper* and anything from three to five destroyers. A formidable foe. Both *Sheffield* and *Jamaica* occasionally disappeared behind columns of climbing water as the German salvos straddled them, each salvo (had it scored a hit) capable of smashing the cruisers. The British ships were firing at tremendous speed—a salvo every twenty-five seconds—but there was the growing threat of a torpedo attack from the destroyers.

Burnett decided to turn away from this threat and come in from another angle; but at the same moment *Lützow*, perturbed at the fast and accurate fire being maintained at him, also turned away, followed by *Hipper*. The Germans continued on south-west, each moment taking them away from the convoy. Force R shadowed them for a while until it was satisfied that it was not a feint; then Admiral Burnett returned to his main task, the safety of JW51B, and of convoy RA51 which was approaching from the east. The battle was over. JW51B had been saved; it had been fought through, eventually reaching Kola Inlet unscathed, except for one splinter which hit the American ship *Calobre*. Little

Achates, sinking, finally gave up the ghost; in deplorable weather *Northern Gem* clawed her way to the cripple and managed to save most of her crew.

Measured by any yardstick, fighting JW51B through without loss was a complete triumph for the Navy. Captain Sherbrooke in *Onslow* had fought his ship doggedly and bravely, forcing a superior enemy to turn away again and again from the convoy, and the task had been taken over adequately by Commander Kinloch in *Obedient* when *Onslow* was smashed. The losses, measured in cold-blooded terms of men and ships, were light considering the overwhelming weight of armament against them. *Bramble*, shattered, a drifting hulk, had twice forced a heavy cruiser to turn away and had salvaged valuable minutes, minutes which were beyond price. *Achates*, with her smoke-screen bolstering up *Onslow*, *Orwell*, *Obedient* and *Obdurate*, had masked the convoy successfully. A complete triumph.

On a more human note, of the hundreds of distant spectators at Scapa, at Altenfiord and at the Admiralty, watching the fight unfold itself dispassionately on large-scale charts as the terse signals arrived, were two people with personal and intimate concern in the drama. Doing a turn of duty in the Admiralty Operations Room was Mrs. Sherbrooke, wife of *Onslow's* captain. What her thoughts were as the battle unfolded one can only hazard a guess. And at Scapa, grimly watching the development and ultimate success of the battle, was Admiral Sir John Tovey, who in 1917 had also commanded a destroyer named *Onslow*—predecessor to the present ship.

Admiral Burnett and *Sheffield, Jamaica, Onslow* and *Orwell* were some time in the future to help make history in those self-same icy waters, also against a heavy German surface craft, *Scharnhorst*, and also in defence of a JW convoy. But of that, more later.

Sixteen

AFTER the success in fighting through JW51B and the unscathed arrival of JW51A, two more convoys—JW52 and JW53—were sailed within a fortnight, one of fourteen and the other of twenty-eight ships. Then wiser counsels prevailed and the sailings were stopped until the following November. In any event, the war in the Mediterranean and the Atlantic convoys were demanding increasing numbers of merchant ships and warships.

Stalin showed a marked petulance over this temporary abandonment of convoys, and refused to accept the fact that to send convoys through in the endless daylight of summer and early autumn was a needless sacrifice. The Russian leader applied increasing and almost endless pressure on Mr. Churchill to resume the convoys regardless of the losses, and to make them larger and more frequent. The same pressure was also being applied to Mr. Roosevelt, but his view was more remote, more detached. By this time the Germans were in dire straits in Russia; America was beginning to stir forcibly in the Far East; and heavy commitments were looming for Europe. Mr. Roosevelt merely passed on Stalin's pungent comments to Mr. Churchill—who already knew them off by heart.

In fact Mr. Churchill has recorded an astringent note on the brusque, at times rude, manner in which Stalin treated him. Early in January 1943, his patience strained, he wrote to Mr. Anthony Eden following a triangular exchange of notes between the Russian Ambassador in London, M. Maisky, Mr. Eden and Mr. Churchill:

'M. Maisky is not telling the truth when he says I promised Stalin convoys of thirty ships each in January and February. The only promise made in my telegram of December 29th to Stalin informed him that the December PQ convoy (actually JW51A and JW51B) prospered so far beyond expectation that I have now arranged to send a full convoy of thirty ships through in January, though whether they will go in one portion or two is not yet settled by the Admiralty.

(In fact fourteen ships sailed in JW52 on 17 January and twenty-eight ships sailed in JW53 on 15 February. Six ships turned back from JW53 because of bad weather, none was lost through enemy action.—E. B.)

'Maisky should be told [Mr. Churchill continues], that I am getting to the end of my tether with these repeated Russian naggings and that it is not the slightest use trying to knock me about any more. . . .'

So in effect Mr. Churchill's promise was fulfilled, with a few ships to spare by the sailing of JW52 and JW53.

No more convoys were routed to Russia until November 1943, and with the sailing of convoy RA52 on 29 January and RA53 on 1 March in that same year, return convoys also ceased for nine or ten months.

JW52 sailed (by northern convoy standards) with a modest escort under the command of Commander W. H. Selby in the destroyer *Onslaught*.

Many of the destroyers were now equipped with the latest anti-U-boat device, the high-frequency direction-finding equipment, which soon earned itself the sobriquet 'Huff-Duff'. By it cross bearings could be made by ships in an escort of the extremely loquacious submarines which were addicted to lengthy conversations between one another, as well as sending long signals of convoy movements and speeds. Once a series of bearings had been obtained on a chattering submarine or two, and the exact positions established, a convoy could be altered away at nightfall with perhaps a swift counter-attack by an escort in order to drive them below for a time. When finally the submarines surfaced it was to see an open expanse of water entirely bereft of ships.

Commander Selby in *Onslaught* and Vice-Admiral Sir Malcolm Goldsmith, the Commodore, played tag with the U-boats, and JW52 arrived safely to face only a dispirited attack by a few torpedo-bombers in the Barents Sea, and which produced nothing and cost the Germans two planes. The hard-worked but jubilant escort for JW52 learned that the penalty for doing a job well was to be promptly given another one; so after a couple of days for re-fuelling and catching up on lost sleep, Commander Selby's force set out as escort for RA52—a convoy of eleven ships. One ship was hit by a submarine which had penetrated the screen, but the crew was taken off and the ship sunk by the escort.

When JW53 sailed there was the added problem of the lengthening hours of spring daylight, which made it possible —it was *always* a possibility for every convoy—that German surface raiders would sally out. So a powerful escort was formed. There were *Scylla*, now a regular frequenter of those grim waters, the escort-carrier *Dasher*, and under Captain I. M. R. Campbell in *Milne*, twelve destroyers: *Faulknor*, *Boadicea*, *Inglefield*, another hardy veteran, *Fury* (whose crew had to think hard to remember when she had not had snow on her decks), *Intrepid*, *Impulsive*, the now repaired *Eclipse*, the Polish destroyer *Orkan*, and the battling quartet which had outfought the *Hipper* and *Lützow*—*Orwell*, *Opportune*, *Obedient* and *Obdurate*. Their job was to stay out at a distance and thoroughly discourage any submarines or aircraft. In addition they would not be averse to trying to repeat *Onslow's* epic fight should any surface raider show up.

The destroyers were to join the convoy off Iceland to which spot it would be escorted by the 'close escort' comprising the minesweeper *Jason* under command of Senior Officer Escort, Commander H. G. A. Lewis, three Hunt-class destroyers, *Pytchley*, *Middleton* and *Meynell*, the minesweeper *Halcyon*, the corvettes *Dianella*, *Poppy* and *Bergamot*, and two more long-standing Arctic residents, the trawlers *Lord Middleton* (which made the most of its peerage when exchanging signals with the Hunt-class destroyer *Middleton*) and the *Lord Austin*. February began in a thoroughly boisterous mood which developed into something more lethal and sinister. *Milne*, returning from Loch

Ewe after a convoy conference, took an awful beating en route for Iceland while behind her the convoy was being really savaged. Ship after ship reported damage or else shifting deck cargo which, as usual, consisted of American tanks, railway engines and wagons. Six had to return to harbour for repairs.

The carrier *Dasher*, too, was damaged and had to drop out. With bitter irony her crew, having congratulated themselves that they had escaped one extremely unpleasant job for the time being, had a much more severe shock. She returned to the Clyde for repairs. American-built, British officers had never been completely happy about her petrol storage and distribution system and, tragic to relate, she blew up in the Clyde with a tremendous explosion and heavy loss of life. Admiral Burnett was given the task of providing a cruiser screen with his flag in *Belfast*, and *Sheffield* and *Cumberland* in company. *Sheffield* was damaged by mountainous seas, one of which swept overboard her fore gun-turret. Finally, however the gale died down and the convoy sailed six ships and two escorts short, *Sheffield* and *Dasher*.

The convoy was to miss *Dasher* with her planes. When it was between Jan Mayen Island and Bear Island, forced to a southerly course by the ice, a snooper plane appeared. Because there were no carrier-borne fighters to chase it away or shoot it down, the plane was able to home both U-boats and aircraft on to JW53. The submarines arrived first, but so resolute was the defence—aided by Huff-Duff—that no U-boat got close enough to attack. The convoy was well down the home stretch when the German aircraft appeared. The first attack was made by a round dozen JU88s. It was no surprise, for *Scylla's* radar had given warning and the reception was too hot for the Germans. With the concentrated escorts, the merchant ships and *Scylla* all firing at the same time, there was scarcely room in the sky for a shell to burst or a string of tracer to travel upwards. The bombers pulled away. One further but half-hearted attack the next day was driven off and within a few hours JW53 had arrived. In safety.

For those of the escort force who were not being stationed in Russia it was a short stay indeed. Once again, as with JW52 and RA52, it was simply a matter of arriving, re-fuelling and preparing to sail. This convoy sailed on 1 March and comprised thirty ships. After being at sea four or five days some of the escorts on the starboard side of the convoy could feel the bitterly cold wind sweeping down from the ice, and could at times detect it glistening in the darkness. The convoy altered course to a more southerly line and even then was sailing through pancake ice, ice which lies on the surface of the water with no depth to it and looks, as its name implies, like white pancakes. U-boats loathed pancake ice for it was thick enough to damage a periscope.

No Luftwaffe aircraft appeared, and to the escort's know-ledge they were keeping excellent tabs on the U-boats. One however managed to slip through the screen and fired tor-pedoes into the mass of shipping, hitting two ships, the *Richard Bland* and the *Executive*. The *Richard Bland* was damaged well forward and was still manageable, but the *Executive* was soon on fire and had to be sunk by one of the destroyers. Then the JU88s appeared to take a hand, but without the success afforded to the submarines. They were driven off, some of them smoking badly and limping. No more attacks materialized, but the bad weather did. The convoy was smitten by a real Arctic circle screaming gale, with the inevitable result that the ships in ballast were driven at all angles with the helpless escorts trying their best to shepherd them. And by now some of the destroyers were short of fuel oil, and Captain Campbell had to detach those worst off to Iceland to re-fuel and to rejoin the convoy while another four went off to replenish.

As the weather gradually eased so the wandering sheep were rounded up—most of them, anyway. Eventually twenty-one of the original twenty-eight were gathered once more into columns, and laboured onwards. But the gale had been too much for a Liberty ship *J. L. M. Curry*. She was a welded craft and splits appeared in her seams. These got progressively worse until finally she broke in half and went under. The crew was picked up by the *Lord Austin*. An aircraft appeared out of the murk, identified itself as a Liberator and reported that a small group of ships was fifty miles away. Eventually most of them were rounded up, but a pitiable call came from the *Porto Rican* that a submarine was attacking her. Alas, she was too far away to be helped. Then came the last signal: she had been torpedoed. Another success came the way of the U-boats which were hanging on to the fringe of the still ragged convoy; they found the *Richard Bland* limping along courageously despite her previous damage. She had survived the gale only to fall victim to another torpedo which this time sank her.

Eclipse and *Impulsive* were unable to arrive in time to save her, but they rescued most of her crew. Still searching, they combed the convoy track until they found floating in the water some wreckage which was easily identifiable as coming from a merchant ship. *And in the middle of it, clinging to a small raft no larger than a good-sized dining-table, was one man, alive!* He was the sole survivor of the *Porto Rican*, and he had clung tenaciously to the raft for nearly seventy hours continually swept by the seas, frozen until he was beyond feeling, but his will to live was supreme. . . .

There were no more losses, and finally RA53 limped in, having been joined at the end by another straggler, the *Yorkman*, who had dodged north among the ice to escape the submarines. Despite the losses, the wearied escort crews had reason to congratulate themselves. After nearly a month at sea in the most savage waters in the world, they had convoyed through fifty-eight ships, taking them almost over the enemy's doormat. For a few days they could relax, could sleep without the alarm jarring them into instant action. The ships would be still, not endlessly pitching into frighteningly high seas. . . . There would be comfort and comparative ease—until the next time.

But for ten months there would be no Arctic convoys, either RA or JWA. The fighting and convoying were to be in other waters, and they would be no less grim, with losses and gaps in the ranks; but there would be no ice, no snow and the gales would seem tame in comparison.

It would make a nice change.

Seventeen

ADMIRAL BRUCE FRASER had taken over from Admiral Tovey as C-in-C Home Fleet when the convoys were resumed in November 1943, but their ideas were so markedly similar that the change brought about no material alteration in policy. The convoys had to sail, therefore there had to be powerful escorts, there had to be cruiser screening forces, and in the wings, waiting and watching, there had to be British heavy ships. It was a continuation of the weary, monotonous round in merciless waters, where a brief period of laxity resulted in a dire penalty. And the year passed.

There had been changes, too, in the German High Command. Raeder had given way to that ruthless exponent of the all-in submarine war, Donitz. Hitler, infuriated over the humiliation of *Hipper* and *Lützow* by the much lighter British cruisers, *Sheffield* and *Jamaica*, and the resolute defence of the convoy by Captain Sherbrooke's destroyers, raved. He threatened, too, to reduce all the heavy German ships to the status of training-ships or, worse still, break them for scrap and distribute the men throughout his hard-pressed land forces. Donitz, hitherto an implacable foe of large ships, was also a submarine fanatic, and rather surprisingly proposed in the spring of 1943 that some heavy ships should be stationed in north Norway, presentable targets for them being the Arctic convoys running to Russia! He added that he felt that the severe restrictions placed upon commanding officers to avoid a fight with equal or superior forces should be relaxed.

Donitz had his way, and a redoubtable foe of ours, *Scharnhorst*, was sent north to join *Tirpitz*. Now if any ship was remembered by the Royal Navy with any degree of bitterness it was *Scharnhorst*. It was she who destroyed the *Rawalpindi*. During the evacuation of Narvik, the battle-cruiser had sunk the aircraft-carrier *Glorious*, as well as other ships. In 1941, in a brief two months' foray into the Atlantic, *Scharnhorst* had caused us endless trouble. Finally, her name was engraved in the hearts of naval men by her audacious dash through the Channel. And now *Scharnhorst* was to be added to the ships threatening the Russian convoys!

Possibly the Germans imagined that because we had pushed through succeeding convoys with success that we had permitted a degree of laxity to creep in. Nothing however was farther from the truth.

Towards the end of 1943—20 December to be precise—convoy JW54B was formed and sailed steadily north. In less than forty-eight hours it was inevitably spotted. Admiral Bruce Fraser took to sea on the evening of 23 December aboard *Duke of York*, with the cruiser *Jamaiça,* and a screen of destroyers, *Savage*, *Saumarez*, *Scorpion* and the Norwegian *Stord*. The cruiser screen for the convoy was *Belfast*, *Norfolk* and *Sheffield*.

Christmas Eve came and with it the dubious lift of deteriorating weather. No snooper planes appeared, but submarines had placed themselves on the flanks of the convoy and were reporting its laboured passage. Fortunately they located neither C-in-C in *Duke of York* nor Admiral Burnett's cruisers. With that sixth sense given to some seamen, Admiral Fraser in *Duke of York* and Captain James McCoy, Senior Officer Escort in the destroyer *Onslow*, had a hunch that this convoy would see, or meet, something out of the ordinary. So deep-rooted was this feeling that the Admiral ordered the convoy to turn back on its course for three or four hours. This was a complicated movement for columns of ships in bad weather, but they did it so that the possibility of a surface raider meeting up with the outward-bound convoy was reduced for a few hours until Admiral Fraser could set the stage for his dramatic heavies to make an entrance. A turbulent Christmas Eve passed and went into a weary Christmas Day, and Captain McCoy watchfully waited for the first appearance of a surface raider in the short twilight—so certain was he that one *would* come.

Instead, on orders from C-in-C in *Duke of York*, Captain Campbell in the destroyer *Milne*, escorting convoy RA55A, now reaching the comparatively safer area west of Bear Island, transferred to JW54's escort four hard-bitten Arctic veterans, *Musketeer*, *Matchless*, *Opportune* and *Virago*. Meanwhile, ashore at Altenfiord, the German Naval Staff, informed of JW55B's progress since the snooper plane had spotted it on 22 December, estimated that the evening of the 25th or morning of the 26th would be a suitable time to sail.

The Luftwaffe and U-boats were ordered to probe a wide area all around the convoy before *Scharnhorst* was committed. They located the convoy on a pin-point, but completely failed to spot either *Duke of York* and *Jamaica*, or Admiral Burnett's three cruisers. And *Scharnhorst* sailed on Christmas night. JW55B, its escort the cruiser screen and *Duke of York* and her force, moved eastward in the gale-lashed darkness, rolling and pitching along at around six knots. At times it was scarcely possible to see the next ship ahead, or the one on the beam; but all knew that somewhere in the darkness to south-east and south-west were ships flying the White Ensign, ships waiting for just one signal. And at 0340 hours it came.

Scharnhorst was at sea. The ship which had been more trouble to us than any other German ship was out on the rampage. She had sailed with a screen of three destroyers. She had sailed just as *Tirpitz* had sailed against convoy PQ12 and as *Hipper* and *Lützow* had sailed against JW51B. But for a fantastic trick of fate—a turn to port instead of to starboard—*Tirpitz* would have been trapped by Admiral Tovey in *King George V* and *Duke of York* and *Renown*. The battle of North Cape would have been fought much earlier. The framework of the pattern had remained unchanged except for the weight of gunfire. Now *Duke of York* alone was to face *Scharnhorst* with cruisers in support.

Two hundred miles south-west of the convoy steamed *Duke of York* and *Jamaica* with the destroyers heading eastward. Between forty and fifty miles south-east of the convoy was Force 1—*Belfast*, *Sheffield* and *Norfolk*. Both forces were so placed that as the minutes and hours passed they were closing the only bolt-hole left for *Scharnhorst*, should she turn south and run as *Tirpitz* had done. And north of them convoy JW55B steamed on.

Convoy, Force 1 and *Duke of York* and consorts were the three angles of a triangle; and somewhere within that shrinking triangle might be *Scharnhorst* if she seriously meant to threaten the convoy and ultimately attack it. If that were so then the two British forces would have to concentrate and concert their actions, so that the base line of the triangle would have *Scharnhorst* south of it. But where was *Scharnhorst*? Admiral Bey, a man of different calibre from Ciliax on *Tirpitz* or Admiral Kummetz on *Hipper*, flew his flag from *Scharnhorst* knowing that this was the last chance the German navy would have of justifying itself in the eyes of Hitler.

Once clear of Altenfiord, *Scharnhorst* turned resolutely north to cut the convoy course. During the night she sent her three destroyers questing ahead, fanned out to seek and report the convoy. She knew that a cruiser screening force was supporting the convoy; but she did not know that Fraser was out with Home Fleet units. So the stage was set. Throughout the long, black hours of darkness this mass of shipping in its several parts was being impacted. What passed for daylight began to tinge the blackness with grey—no more than that. *Belfast's* course, north-west, was a punishing one for she was heading into the still savage end of the gale. Shortly before 0900 hours *Belfast's* radar showed one solitary *blip*. Was it *Scharnhorst*? Was it a straggler lost from the convoy? If it was *Scharnhorst* then she had slipped through the screen and was ideally placed for an attack on the convoy. Assuming the convoy had maintained the same speed and course of the past day or two, *Scharnhorst*—if the *blip* was really her—was astride the convoy course and was ahead of it, waiting.

Admiral Burnett punished his ship severely. They increased speed, plunged through solid water which froze as it fell on deck, adding to the ice already forming from the repeated snow-squalls. At 0930 hours a vague, bulky shadow loomed out of the murk. And was identified. *Scharnhorst!* But Burnett had out-manœuvred her; he was between her and the convoy. *Belfast* opened fire with star shells which outlined the looming German ship, and *Norfolk* and *Sheffield* hit at her with crashing broadsides. The battle-cruiser did not open fire in return, but drastically altered course, turning south where, unknown to Admiral Bey, Fraser was stopping the bolt-hole.

Admiral Burnett, experienced veteran of cruiser screens on Arctic convoys, kept his primary task well to the forefront of his mind—that of the safety of the convoy. He shrewdly assessed that *Scharnhorst*, convinced that she was facing only one or two light cruisers, would turn again to hit the convoy. He signalled that he was in action with *Scharnhorst*, but *Duke of York* maintained silence. Burnett could only hope that Admiral Fraser was listening and in a position to join in. His shrewd assessment of *Scharnhorst's* manœuvre was accurate. The German ship had turned south from the first attack, then east and northwards again, still bent on destroying the convoy and, if possible, the cruisers. When she approached for the second time at about 1230 hours *Belfast*, *Norfolk* and *Sheffield* were admirably placed on the bow of the convoy.

Burnett did not hesitate. The three cruisers turned in line abreast and went hell-for-leather full speed straight at *Scharnhorst* firing as hard as they could. For a few minutes *Scharnhorst* maintained the same course and it looked as if the three cruisers had a fight on their hands. Then she turned away once more, increased speed and tore off into the concealing murk. Along her length, as she turned, the pursuing ships could seen pin-points of red light as their shells struck home. *Scharnhorst* had realized by now that she was opposed by more than one cruiser, and she feared that somewhere in that murk were some British destroyers with their dreaded torpedoes. Her guns flashed as she increased speed to get away from the cruisers. And *Norfolk* was hit.

What Burnett had schemed for was turning out to perfection. The battle-cruiser was being forced away from the convoy, compelled to steam south where, Burnett hoped, *Duke of York* was waiting. As the convoy, after an emergency turn north for a brief interval, resumed its easterly course the cruisers shadowed *Scharnhorst* by radar. Wriggle and twist as she might they still held her in their green glinting screens. *Scharnhorst* had completely lost touch with her destroyers. As a matter of fact they had cut across the convoy's course, continued on northwards and were feverishly combing the empty sea with a convoy, the cruisers and *Duke of York* with her destroyers between them and home.

But while this was going on, where were the *Duke of York* and *Jamaica*? South of the action, maintaining a firm course of 080 degrees, slightly north of east, and a steady speed of twenty-six knots. This was a punishing pace for the destroyers, and no tribute can be too high to their captains—and their coxswains—for keeping position in that heavy following sea.

Now comes a sidelight which if used in fiction would be dismissed with scornful laughter. The cruisers, still shadowing the southbound *Scharnhorst*, were reporting her at intervals to *Duke of York*. Nobody but Fraser knew whereabouts his squadron was, what course or speed it was steering, or if it was in a position to hit the German ship. At the Admiralty heads were concentrated over the large-scale chart. There was the convoy clearly marked, there was Force 1 clearly marked shadowing *Scharnhorst* which also was clearly marked. But where was *Duke of York*? Was this to be another narrow escape for the German raider? Was she to slip through the net as *Tirpitz* had done?

On *Duke of York's* bridge an anxious conference was taking place. Admiral Fraser knew that soon he would be taking the ship into action. The long afternoon, now shrouded in darkness, had closed down over the ships. It was 1600 hours. On *Duke of York's* radar *Scharnhorst* appeared, forty miles distant, less than an hour's steaming time. So, the conference had to decide. Tea before action or after? It broke up—a decision made. *Duke of York* would take tea before action.

At 1630 hours, tea disposed of, the warning action gongs on *Duke of York* clanged out. *Scharnhorst* was on the port bow, seven miles away. Behind her, eight miles astern, *Belfast* still shadowed, holding her in the inexorable radar, reporting her every move. Admiral Fraser knew that *Scharnhorst* was completely unaware that heavy British units were near her. He decided to hold his fire until the enemy could be illuminated by star shell. The range closed. The big German plunged into the heavy seas, gaining all the time on the faithful *Belfast*. Then suddenly in plain language to *Belfast* went the signal: 'Illuminate the enemy with star shell.'

The *Duke of York* had arrived—the giants were in the ring together. *Belfast's* guns spoke, then high above the German ship the star shells shattered the wind- and snow-lashed darkness. Silhouetted against the black background *Scharnhorst* stood out starkly, a black mass with a white pile of water around her bows. Now it was *Duke of York's* turn. Admiral Fraser spoke to the Captain, the Captain spoke to his Gunnery Officer, the Gunnery Officer spoke to his guns' crews waiting on the 14-inch guns. No voice was raised more than a hair's-breadth above the conversational tone—and *Duke of York* was framed in flame as her guns hurled their three-quarter of a ton projectiles through the air. She rolled and shuddered, and Admiral Fraser came near to injury in the first minutes of the fight, for the heavy brass bridge-clock, shaken from its fastenings, fell, missing him by inches.

Duke of York was right for line in the first salvo, and

there was at least one hit. Then *Scharnhorst* replied. Her side was lit by sudden flashes of orange and her shells tore over *Duke of York* in rapid climbing crescendoes like a train rumbling through a station. The German ship turned, wriggling and twisting, firing back, and around 1800 hours on that wild evening it looked as if she were going to escape final retribution. She increased her speed and opened the range to more than 20,000 yards, more than ten miles. Unknown to Admiral Fraser, however, *Scharnhorst* was more damaged than had been realized by the British forces. Tearing after her, taking terrific punishment, slammed British destroyers, but it was still a shade over evens that the German ship would wriggle through the trap. Then Instructor-Commander Fleming, who had been correlating the complicated plot to the radar reports, announced quietly, in a voice completely devoid of any excitement or emotion: '*Scharnhorst* has reduced speed to twenty knots.' The trap was finally sprung, with the victim inside.

And what helped to spring it, if incorporated into fiction, would be laughed out of court. One of *Scharnhorst's* shells tore through *Duke of York's* wireless aerials, so that she was unable to speak to the destroyers or shadowing cruisers. Without the attack by the destroyers *Scharnhorst* might well have escaped. Lashed by wind and heavy spray, which was ice by the time it reached him, Lieutenant H. J. R. Bates climbed aloft until he reached the whipping, flaying ends of the aerial. Roughly joining them together, he held them until the vital signal was passed to the destroyers. The destroyers *Savage, Saumarez, Scorpion* and *Stord* had plunged ahead of *Scharnhorst*, even though she was outpacing *Duke of York*. On the bridge and in the radar office on the battleship they watched with bated breath, and with unqualified admiration, the attack carried out by the destroyers on the German raider. *Scharnhorst* and the four destroyers were but pale green blobs on the radar screens, but it was drama of the most intense kind. Three thousand yards, 2,500, 2,000 yards . . . the destroyers thrust inwards, risking destruction at that range by *Scharnhorst's* secondary armament. The range was too great for *Duke of York* to give them any help. For the time being it was their fight.

Savage and *Saumarez* tore in on the starboard side of the desperately wriggling enemy, and *Scorpion* and *Stord* swept in on the port side, their 40,000-h.p. engines straining to get every ounce of power from the racing screws. They came under a merciless fire from *Scharnhorst's* secondary armament, without being hit. They fired their torpedoes and turned away, a task well done behind them. Aboard the destroyers and *Duke of York* could be felt three distinct thuds transmitted through the water—three torpedoes had struck.

It was at this point that Commander Fleming had reported that the enemy had slowed down to twenty-knots. *Duke of York* overhauled the *Scharnhorst* again, as her speed was reported to be dropping . . . fifteen knots . . . ten knots. Then she was virtually at a standstill; but orange-red flashes from her decks showed that she was still fighting like a cornered wolf. Admiral Fraser ordered the faithful *Belfast* to close in and fire torpedoes. She did so and scored one hit. In the meantime *Duke of York* again opened fire and deluged *Scharnhorst* with 14-inch shells, while *Jamaica* closed in to almost point-blank range and pumped in salvo after salvo of 6-inch shells. On board *Scharnhorst* fires blazed like infernos, both forward and aft, yet still her guns thundered back defiantly. As *Jamaica* hammered at her from one side, *Belfast*, *Sheffield* and *Norfolk* closed in on the other, the flash of their salvos momentarily lighting up the ships.

Weaving through them, like excited terriors around large dogs scrapping together, were the destroyers (among them *Onslow* and *Orwell*) seeking to get in yet another torpedo attack. The situation had its alarming possibilities, however—too easy was it for a friend to loom up in the darkness, her guns bellowing, and another friend mistaking her for, say, one of the absent German destroyers. Then came the voice of authority. Admiral Fraser signalled: 'Clear the area of the target except for those ships with torpedoes, and one destroyer with searchlight.'

Senior Officer destroyers ordered away all his ships except one, which sent the stabbing white fan of her searchlight across the water, and for the first time the crippled *Scharnhorst* was revealed. She was listing heavily, flames gouted from her at a dozen different points. *Jamaica* closed in for the kill. A salvo of torpedoes leapt from her tubes. There was an interval of waiting, then tremendous explosions rent the air, and flame and smoke temporarily concealed the stricken monster. When the smoke cleared away *Scharnhorst* was seen to be lying on her side. It was the death throes—the end was only a matter of minutes.

Duke of York turned from the scene, her task completed. As she did so Admiral Fraser signalled destroyers to go in and pick up survivors; and from the water they picked stunned and wounded men—then they, too, turned away, leaving the sinking *Scharnhorst* to disappear beneath the icy waters.

The Battle of the North Cape was over.

Epilogue

FROM the 15 November 1943, when the convoys were resumed with JW54B, up to the final convoy in May 1945, seventeen more convoys were thrust through. And out of those seventeen convoys, only five ships were lost by enemy action. Between them rather more than 360 ships were convoyed outwards, and approximately the same number home. The RA convoys lost eight ships. A sum total of thirteen ships lost in fourteen convoys.

Admiral Ruge, a noted German writer on naval affairs, writing of Anglo-American sea-power and its effect on the land war in Europe, wrote:

'Between August 1944 and April 1955 the ships on the Arctic run carried over a million tons of war material. The weapons, equipment and vehicles allowed Russia to equip a further sixty motorized divisions. . . .'

The Admiral's estimate covers a period in which only eight convoys sailed for Russia, JWS 59 to 66. In actual fact, between the sailing of the first true convoy, PQ1, on 9 September 1941 and the last, JW67, on 12 May 1945, nearly 1,000 ships sailed outwards for Russia, carrying material amounting to between five and six million tons.

Alas, not all of it arrived. In terms of cold cash the value of the material carried in this joint Anglo-American project amounted to £430,000,000. This included 5,000 tanks, 7,000 aircraft, twelve complete freight trains with engines, hundreds of thousands of tons of high explosive and high-octane spirit, and medical supplies which the Russians assiduously steered away from our sick and wounded.

From the outward-bound convoys sixty-two merchant ships were lost—half of them from two convoys, PQ17 and PQ18; and of the return convoys twenty-eight ships never made port. After the holocaust of PQ17 and PQ18, when the convoy letters were altered to JW, convoys sailed outwards and lost only five ships, three from JW56 and two from JW65.

These figures may tempt one to imagine that in the later stages the run became easier, that the Royal Navy had got the Arctic run nicely buttoned-up. The increased size of escorts, the later fitting of anti-aircraft guns, anti-aircraft ships and carriers had much to do with the reduced losses, of course, and later escorts, immeasurably stronger and better armed, were able to hit back and hit hard. The Germans lost thirty-two submarines and well over a hundred aircraft in their attacks on the convoys. But our naval losses were severe, too—two cruisers, six destroyers, three sloops, two frigates, three corvettes, and three minesweepers with a consequent loss of 1,840 men who have no known grave.

How heavy were the demands made on our naval forces—at a time when the drain from other theatres of war were enormous—can be assessed from the following figures.

Between 1941 and 1945 the Royal Navy called on more than 200 warships of various kinds to form escorts drawn from eight light cruisers, four anti-aircraft cruisers, four anti-aircraft ships, converted merchant ships, fourteen escort-carriers, 102 destroyers, seventeen fleet sweepers, eighteen sloops and frigates, twenty-four corvettes and seventeen asdic trawlers. A formidable fleet.

It is to my great regret that I cannot give the names of every ship, the commanding officers, officers and men aboard them. And I ask no pardon for paraphrasing Sir Winston Churchill's words used in connection with another war sphere: 'When people talk of the convoys to Russia they can lift high their heads and say "I was there". Lift them high with pride.'

It was a true Anglo-American operation because while most of the escorts were British, the majority of the ships in the convoy were American owned and American manned.

To the best of my knowledge there is no known monument to those who died, the 1,840 British naval personnel, nor to the hundreds of merchant seamen who perished.

I would like to see a simple monument erected to them facing north on North Cape, facing the waters in which they questioned not the giving, but in fulfilment of a promise they gave—and gave their all.

Age shall not weary them
Nor the years condemn . . .

Only the bitter northern seas remain the same. Antagonists in life, British, American, French and German, lie beneath those cold waters with only the shriek of a gale for their requiem, and the freezing sea for their shroud.

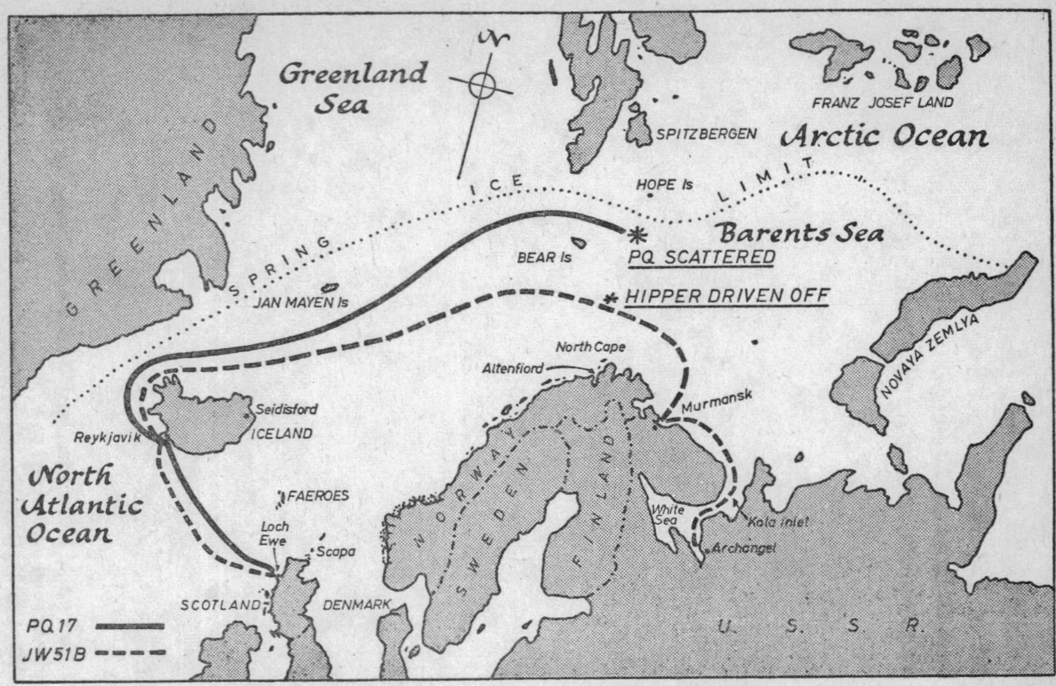
Greenland Sea
FRANZ JOSEF LAND
SPITZBERGEN
Arctic Ocean
GREENLAND
SPRING ICE LIMIT
HOPE Is
Barents Sea
BEAR Is
PQ SCATTERED
JAN MAYEN Is
HIPPER DRIVEN OFF
NOVAYA ZEMLYA
North Cape
Altenfiord
Murmansk
Seidisford
ICELAND
Reykjavik
North Atlantic Ocean
FAEROES
NORWAY
SWEDEN
FINLAND
White Sea
Kola inlet
Archangel
Loch Ewe
Scapa
SCOTLAND
DENMARK
U. S. S. R.
PQ17
JW51B